THE THEORY AND PRACTICE OF CORBYNISM

Neil Schofield-Hughes

Table of Contents

INTRODUCTION

In the summer of 2015, following a catastrophic general election defeat, the Labour Party – wholly unpredictability – elected the veteran Left-wing backbencher Jeremy Corbyn as its leader. After a year in which his Parliamentary Party passed a no-confidence vote and most of his Shadow Cabinet resigned, Corbyn was re-elected in the summer of 2016 by an increased margin, comfortably seeing off a challenge from Owen Smith. And in June 2017, Corbyn's Labour Party hugely out-performed expectations in a general election called by Conservative Prime Minister Theresa May in the expectation of wiping out a fractured Labour opposition, depriving her of her Commons majority.

Since Corbyn was first elected, there has been much argument about what Corbyn represents, and what his period as Labour leader tells us about his Party and about the nature of UK Labour politics.

Following his election, Jeremy Corbyn promised that there would be a new style and method of politics. The purpose of this book is to offer a critical examination of the politics of the Labour Party following the election of Jeremy Corbyn as leader in 2015. It attempts to answer a number of questions, in particular:

- What is the philosophical and intellectual basis of Corbynism?
- What is its position within the political tradition of the UK Labour Party?
- What models of party politics does it espouse?
- What does it tell us about the nature of UK politics at a difficult time?
- Who are the Corbynists? What are their political aspirations?

Above all, how does Corbynism fit into a period which has seen, among other things, a crisis of social democracy; a resurgence of the nationalist right, both in Britain and around the world; a collapse in faith in the institutions of British Parliamentary democracy?

And, ultimately, all of these beg the question of whether there is any such thing as Corbynism, and, if so, what is it – and in what way does it approach the main political issues of the day?

It's difficult sometimes to get a clear view of the ideological and practical nature of Corbyn's Labour, as it provokes extremes of vilification and admiration. The vilification – from the right-wing press in particular – is obvious; Corbyn is a man who snubbed the Queen, who made common cause with the IRA and Hezbollah, who refused to sing the National Anthem. The adulation is equally extreme – a man of principle who has always been on the right side of history, untainted by the red Toryism of Blair, a lifelong anti-racist, a man some of whose supporters have – wholly without irony – dubbed a political Dumbledore, a wise old man who alone has the integrity and ideas to effect a transformation of society for the many.

Underlying all of this is the assumption that the election of Jeremy Corbyn marked a decisive change within Labour Party politics. Since that election in 2015, the Labour Party has undergone some fairly fundamental changes – not least the huge expansion of its membership, and some key changes in the way in which the Party has been organised. It has been tested electorally both by the referendum on membership of the European Union in 2016 but, most notably, in the General Election of 2017 – a snap election called by a Conservative Prime Minister who was confident of receiving a strong electoral mandate for her vision of Brexit and in which, against all predictions, Jeremy Corbyn's Labour Party made significant gains and deprived the Conservatives of their majority.

At the same time, the 2016 referendum result has presented major policy challenges to the Corbyn leadership, and more recently the need to deal with serious allegations of anti-Semitism on the Labour Left has thrown up both significant organisational challenges as well as raising profound questions about the Labour Party's commitment to oppose racism.

There are deeper questions, too. This book therefore aims to consider how the practice of Corbynism within the Labour Party is intellectually and philosophically grounded, as well as offering a view on the traditions that Corbyn and Corbynism represents.

This book is not meant as a history or a chronology. It aims to look critically behind events at the ideas and political traditions that Corbyn's Labour draws on, and how it operates in practise. It asks questions about the origins of Corbynism, its political heritage, the politics that have driven the creation of a mass party – as well as considering those key issues of Brexit and antisemitism, both of which provide illuminating case studies of both the ideology and praxis of the Labour Party under Corbyn.

Three general points need to be made about this book.

First, I am writing this in the summer of 2018, when a number of key issues that I discuss are still very much alive – notably Brexit and the arguments surrounding institutional antisemitism in the Labour Party. It appears likely that in both cases there will be significant developments in the latter part of 2018. But the important thing – at this point – is to understand why the Labour Party leadership has taken up the positions that it has, and how those positions reflect its values.

British politics is currently dominated by the issue of leaving the European Union – Brexit – which, a little over six months before the final exit date, and a matter of weeks before the date by which a deal has to be finalised, remains unresolved and in deadlock. Both main political parties are split on the issue; there is every indication that there will be a serious political crisis in the coming autumn, on that has the potential to split both major parties and could even lead to a fundamental realignment in the British party system.

Within the Labour Party, the issue of Brexit remains deeply divisive. The Labour Party's leadership's line is still to support the idea of Brexit – on the grounds that the will of the people expressed in the referendum must be respected - while arguing that the UK should negotiate a "jobs first" Brexit by negotiating a bespoke customs and market agreement with the EU, in which the UK is not a rule-taker and elements of EU regulation that would inhibit the implementation of Labour's domestic programme would not apply. The majority of Labour-held Parliamentary constituencies voted to leave the EU. On the other hand the majority of Labour's members – on the basis of opinion poll evidence – appear to favour Britiain's continued membership of the EU. Pressure is growing, both inside the Labour Party and outside, for a "people's vote" on any deal, which would include the option of staying inside the EU; the leadership has made it clear that it does not support a second referendum, arguing instead for a "meaningful vote" in Parliament. It is possible – but by no means certain - that there will be a vote on the issue at this Autumn's Labour Party Conference.

On antisemitism, it will be difficult to gauge where Labour is headed until the results are announced of this summer's elections to the National Executive Committee, and one is able to judge whether the crisis around antisemitism will fade away or be intensified. Once again, though, the route to the current impasse is illustrative of the Corbynist mindset, and the way in which Corbyn and his leadership team have handled the issue to date is deeply instructive. Chapter 9 concentrates on those aspects of the issue.

Second, this book is not written from a neutral or academic position. I am a Labour Party member, and a former Labour Party council candidate; I believe in what I regard as core Labour values – fairness, equality, democracy, sustainability, internationalism – and I believe that, historically, the Labour Party, for all its faults and inconsistencies, remains the best political vehicle for achieving those things in Britain. This book will draw on my own personal political experience, both in Brighton and Hove – specifically in the Brighton Pavilion Parliamentary Constituency - where I was a Labour local government candidate in 2015; and more recently in Wales, where I now live and am a member (and, until recently, a General Committee delegate for my ward) of the Cardiff West Constituency Labour Party.

I believe that one of the reasons why the Labour Party has been such an effective vehicle is because it has, unequivocally, been a broad church drawing on a variety of traditions – Methodism as much as Marxism, traditions of ethical liberalism, and because of its organic links with the Trade Union movement. I remain proud of what Labour has achieved – after 1945 in establishing the welfare state, in government in the 1960s in liberalising British society through reforming social measures such as the legalisation of abortion and homosexuality, laying the ground to make Britain a more generous society; and in the years from 1997 to 2010, in reducing child poverty, in establishing the minimum wage, in legalising civil partnerships, in investing in health and education.

That does not mean that I am uncritical of New Labour – there were quite obviously serious failures, of which Blair's decision to go to war in Iraq and the reforms to social security legislation are among the worst, and one can argue that, even in the early stages bolstered by an unprecedented Parliamentary majority, Labour lacked the nerve to carry through key parts of its programme to their logical conclusion; that it was too ready to substitute market disciplines for achieving change through the power of the state. I will be strongly critical of the policy directions Labour took in opposition between 2010 and 2015, and in particular its failure to understand that the economic crash meant that the fundamental approach of Blairite economics – the ability to use growth to fund improved social provision without wholescale redistribution – was no longer a credible option. This point is explored in detail in Chapter 2. But, nonetheless, I believe that the Britain that existed when Labour left office in 2010 was an immeasurably better place than it would have been if the Tories had been in office; and in particular that Gordon Brown's response to the economic crisis of 2008, had it been followed through after 2010, would have avoided the austerity shock that the Tories chose to administer in Government.

Third – and most importantly – I have used "Corbynism" throughout as a shorthand term for the kind of Labour Party that has come into being since 2015. The Labour Party is not a homogenous organisation and there remain a significant number of members who resist and strongly oppose aspects of the party's policy, positioning and practise under Corbyn's leadership. But – especially since that unexpected General Election result in 2017 – it seems clear that no Labour leader has enjoyed the degree of ideological and organisational hegemony that Corbyn now wields. Corbyn the man and the Corbynist party are not the same thing – although it is difficult to think of any British political party in modern times – even Thatcher's Conservative Party – whose public profile is so wholly expressed in terms of its leader. The two must be considered together.

Finally, this book has been written rapidly, and has drawn on my long-standing political blog Notes from a Broken Society[1]. Nearly all the material here is new, but there are brief passages that have been reworked from the blog.

While – obviously – I take full responsibility for everything that is included in the book, it would not have been possible without the support and love of my wife and political comrade, Siân Schofield-Hughes (who, to be fair, recognised the Leninist tendencies of Corbyn's Labour long before I did). And it is to Siân that this book is dedicated, with love and affection.

Neil Schofield-Hughes
Cardiff
August 2018

---

[1] https://notesbrokensociety.wordpress.com/

LABOUR IN OPPOSITION
2010-2015

Jeremy Corbyn's election as Labour leader in 2015 is best understood as an insurgency that reflected a deep and real frustration among an enormous number of people, many of them in the Labour Party, and even more outside. The leadership election can be seen as a sort of political lightning rod, earthing a number of political frustrations that had been steadily building in the preceding years. So to understand the roots of that victory, one needs to look, not just at the election campaign, but the events that led up to that General Election result, and the impact that it had on Labour Party members and activists.

In 2015, Labour had lost an election that it felt it should have won. There can be few Labour people who will forget the trauma of that exit poll on 7th May 2015, after an election campaign in which Labour confidently expected to make gains and potentially to be in Government – if not necessarily majority Government. Despair at that defeat – and the sense of impotence arising from the fact that after everything that had happened during five years of savage austerity – of falling living standards, especially for those who were already the poorest; of the inability of the Conservative-led coalition even to deliver on its own terms, as debt continued to rise; and years of systematic cuts in benefits – Labour could not only not break through, but had actually gone backward in electoral terms; thanks to the collapse in the Liberal Democrat vote, the Tories had gained the majority that eluded them in 2010.

Indeed, the 2015 General Election result was the latest in a sequence of elections that had seen the Labour vote decline from its peak in 1997, when Tony Blair's New Labour government was elected by a landslide. In 1997 Labour won 13.5 million votes – or 43.2 per cent of the vote. By 2010 that had declined to 8.6 million votes, or just over 29% of the vote. In 2015 there had been a small recovery, but only to 9.35 million votes, or 30.4 per cent of the vote[2].

Understanding what had happened in the five years since Labour left office is crucial to appreciating why, only four months after Labour left office, Jeremy Corbyn won the leadership of the Labour Party by a landslide.

Following the economic crash of 2007-8, the long period of Labour rule that began with Tony Blair's 1997 landslide came to an end. It was replaced by a coalition between the Conservatives (who had been expecting to win a landslide themselves, but were unable to win a majority) and a Liberal Democrat party that had moved steadily to the Right on economic issues, under the influence of the so-called Orange Group, a collection of economic liberals who rejected the social liberalism towards which their party had been moving ever since the 1970s. Between them, they instituted a savage policy of economic austerity - focussing on the increase in Government debt that had occurred since the crash - in order, as they put it, to bring the public finances under control and to avert what they presented as a financial crisis.

The central narrative of this new, pro-austerity Government was that it needed to cut public expenditure because the financial crisis had been caused by Labour's overspending in office. The empirical evidence showed that this was not the case[3] - in the early years of the Blair government the Chancellor, Gordon Brown, used buoyant tax revenues to repay national debt and, overall, Government borrowing was no more than average over the Labour years. Moreover - and leaving aside the off-book use of the Private Finance initiative, much of that deficit was used to finance investment at a time when the Private sector was notably failing to do so - for example in health and education infrastructure, which had the effect of creating jobs and boosting the economy while the private sector was locked in a cycle of low investment and falling productivity. The main cause of the huge increase in Government debt after 2007-8 was not profligate social spending, but a combination of the costs of recapitalising the banking system and a collapse in tax revenues following the slump.

---

[2]   https://researchbriefings.parliament.uk/ResearchBriefing/Summary/CBP-7529#fullreport

[3] See, for example, the writings of Professor Simon Wren-Lewis, especially https://mainlymacro.blogspot.com/2013/06/must-we-live-with-post-truth-media.html **and** https://mainlymacro.blogspot.com/2013/06/more-on-myth-of-labour-profligacy.html

However, faced with Tory cuts - and the homely language in which Chancellor George Osborne framed them (maxing out the nation's credit card, mending the roof while the sun shone), Labour in opposition never opposed the myth of overspending in office. Indeed, the myth was compounded by the deeply ill-judged note left on his desk by the outgoing Labour Chief Secretary to the Treasury, Liam Byrne, to the effect that there was no money left[4]; a note that haunted Labour throughout the Parliament that followed. There followed five years in which the Coalition imposed a version of austerity without any significant intellectual opposition from the Labour Party, least of all from shadow Chancellor Ed Balls, who – despite an earlier reputation as an expansionist Keynsian – sounded like a man haunted by the spectre of Labour's economic record as a "tax and spend" party.

Moreover, the language in which they did so was one of necessity - the language of saving the British economy after Labour's mismanagement, in terms powerfully reminiscent of Margaret Thatcher's claim that there was no alternative. And in doing so, they successfully covered the fact that austerity was not a matter of economic necessity, but of *political choice*: there was always an alternative (the fact that total Government debt nearly doubled during the Coalition period of office [reference] is itself testimony to the fact that austerity was not only not a matter of economic necessity, but - by depressing wages and hence tax receipts, and shifting the burden of reward from wages to rents on assets - was actually incapable of achieving its objective of reducing debt). And, after the initial shock of 2007-8, there was little indication that Labour in opposition understood - or at least articulated - the risk associated with private debt as distinct from public deficits; least of all in the context of how the Coalition's deficit reduction strategy quite explicitly represented turning some of the public debt into private debt. (It is ironic that the most consistent political voice warning of the dangers of increasing private debt in the pre-crash years – Liberal Democrat Vince Cable – was now a senior member of a government that appeared quite wilfully determined not to heed those lessons).

The opposition to austerity was sharpened by a belief that while the most vulnerable in society were bearing the brunt of austerity, those who had caused the crash – the bankers – were not only getting away without any pain, but had been bailed out by the Government. It's important to understand that the original plan introduced by Gordon Brown and Alistair Darling was not a bail out, but a recapitalization with clear terms attached; it was the Coalition Government that

---

4 https://www.theguardian.com/commentisfree/2015/may/09/liam-byrne-apology-letter-there-is-no-money-labour-general-election

decided not to make the fundamental reforms of the banking system that Brown and Darling had intended as part of the package[5]. But, in the general sense of unfairness, this nuance was lost; Labour in Government was regarded as culpable for the bail-out.

Anyone who was active in that 2015 Election Campaign knew that the economy was Labour's downfall. Doorstep experience powerfully reinforces the evidence of opinion polling – that Labour was simply not trusted to manage the economy. And, crucially, this had followed five years in which Labour's leadership – most of all in the person of Shadow Chancellor Ed Balls, who was to lose his seat in that election – had argued that Labour had to curb its natural economic instincts in order to make itself electable. But, as the ballot boxes were opened, it was obvious that this strategy had failed – confirming those doorstep experiences.

And a tactic of simply responding to Tory austerity failed to ask the big economic questions, and to develop economic narratives around which Labour could unite. The aftermath of the crash of 2007-8 and the long recession that followed it, during which living standards in the United Kingdom fell further and for longer than at any time since the 1870s, raised further questions about the status of capitalism itself. As austerity bit, the questions started to be asked about whether the fundamental deal at the heart of capitalism – that one could, by selling one's labour, achieve a decent sufficiency for oneself and one's family – still applied. Questions were also asked about the longer term issues like the combination of recession and soaring costs of living, especially housing; of how it was possible that people increasingly could not afford to buy the sort of homes they grew up in, and how the dream of home ownership – a talisman of the popular capitalism of the Thatcher era – had turned sour. The age of being able to buy a suburban semi-detached house on the wage of a skilled worker had long receded. An understanding was growing that the price of rising house prices was a net transfer of wealth, not just from the wage-earners to property-owners, but from the young and poor to the old and (relatively) rich.

---

[5] This issue is dealt with in detail in Brown, Gordon *My Life Our Times* (2017)

[6] Paul Krugman's New York Times column describes the outline https://krugman.blogs.nytimes.com/2013/11/16/secular-stagnation-coalmines-bubbles-and-larry-summers/?smid=fb-share . Sadly Larry Summers' original slides in which he outlines his work appear no longer to be available online.

At the same time, rhetoric about work being the most effective route out of poverty looked hollow in an age in which increasing numbers of people in work were in receipt of benefits – and were being hit hard by the benefit cuts imposed by the coalition.

And, in terms of economic theory, the question was being raised of whether Western economies had entered a phase of what was described as "secular stagnation[6]", in which it was only possible to provide full employment by running dangerous levels of deficit; and that this was one reason why, following the largely benign economic period from 1945-1973, economic crises were becoming more frequent and more severe. Far from being a self-adjusting mechanism in which market forces produced equilibrium and hence stability, the world economy appeared increasingly to be inherently unstable; the neoliberal faith in benign markets that characterized the politics of the 1980s onwards was looking distinctly threadbare, and protest movements were increasingly challenging the basis of a globalized market economy that dominated the political and economic rhetoric of the time.

In other words, the 2008 crash and the long recession that followed it inevitably begged questions about whether we were witnessing the inevitable collapse of capitalism that Marx had foreseen. Writers like Paul Mason – admittedly not a professional economist but a respected journalist who had extensively covered the economic crash and the banking crisis that surrounded it – popularised the idea that there was a fundamental crisis at the heart of capitalism. The harshness of austerity – and the belief that it was a wholly unnecessary reaction to a crisis that came about as a result the crisis of a greed-based, out-of-control international financial system – inevitably led to greater questioning of the concept of what was increasingly known as "neoliberalism".

On two other key issues, Labour in opposition allowed the Coalition to dictate the framing of the political debate, in the name of electability: immigration and social security. On the former, the Labour Party was paralysed by what it saw as the instinct of working class Labour voters; it saw in the immigration issue a rationalisation for its perplexity at a significant fall in votes in its heartlands. There was a period when prominent Labour MPs in particular were calling for an "honest" debate on immigration, when what they really appeared to want was the opportunity to let racist tropes go unchallenged. A truly honest debate on immigration would have included the fact that immigration was good for the economy; that, contrary to tabloid narratives, immigrants globally paid more into the Exchequer in tax than they received in benefits; that many crucial jobs were undertaken by immigrant labour (including in the NHS) in the face of labour shortages at home. In short, rather than accepting tabloid myths about immigrants taking British jobs and drawing generous benefits - let alone stories about mass illegal immigration - a genuinely courageous Labour opposition would have been challenging them, and undermining the rise of the Right by telling the truth. But, especially on the Labour Right, there was no appetite to challenge tabloid mythology; often such activists sought to close down debate with language strikingly reminiscent of Margaret Thatcher's[7] notorious (and unevidenced) claim that many people were afraid of being "swamped"[8] by people from an alien culture..

The nadir was reached during the 2015 election campaign when the Labour Party nationally produced a mug for sale, one of a series depicting Labour's core electoral slogans at £5 a time, printed with the slogan "Controls on Immigration". It caused a furore within the Labour Party – condemned by prominent figures like Diane Abbot but also causing untold offence to party activists[9]. Some constituency Labour Parties refused to distribute it. And in practical terms Labour had the worst of all possible worlds; many people recoiled from the intellectual dishonesty of the position on immigration while there was no real evidence that its adoption of Tory language shored up its vote. The lesson that Labour is at its weakest when it tries to out-Tory the Tories appeared largely to have been lost.

Moreover, Labour's official rhetoric on immigration – and its refusal to argue honestly in the face of what it perceived as "authentic" working-class attitudes to immigration, was deeply patronizing, It appeared to assume that working-class people were incapable of understanding a fact-based approach to immigration; that even a slightly-nuanced economic argument was beyond the people that Labour represented. And as such it appeared to betray what Labour had long stood for.

---

[7] https://www.margaretthatcher.org/document/103485

[8] I myself was on the receivng end one of the more enterprising attempts to close down the debate when I was told by a Labour Party activist that I was "too middle class" to have a legitimate view on immigration. As the gentleman concerned was not known for his intellectual approach to politics he might have been surprised to learn that he was effectively referencing Lenin (but see chapter [x] below).

[9] https://www.independent.co.uk/news/uk/politics/generalelection/labours-diane-abbott-condemns-partys-anti-immigration-mug-as-shameful-10142149.html

Much the same is true of the debate about social security, where the Coalition war on welfare was in essence a continuation of themes that had been laid down under the last years of New Labour.

Indeed, Labour had acquiesced in the increasing use a particularly obnoxious form of political terminology – that of securing the interest of "hard-working families". It was obnoxious and, for Labour, counter-productive, for two reasons:

First, It rested on a particular model of citizenship, defining those who matter as those who are economically active or who lead their lives in a particular way. Doubtless Ed Miliband had no intention of leaving those who couldn't find work, or were too sick to work, out of his vision; or that he wanted to exclude those who live alone, those who had been estranged from their families, those for whom family life was a source of pain and abuse. But that was the effect of the rhetoric; at a time when Miliband was talking at length about "One Nation Labour", it excluded rather than included.

Second, it undermined Labour's strongest economic arguments around the cost of living crisis – about how real wages were falling and how there had been a long-term shift in income from wage-earners to rentiers. Labour liked to talk about making work pay and being the party of work, but while it was happy to talk about "hard working families" it was wholly accepting the Tory framing of the debate. Labour was quite explicitly accepting their assumptions about citizenship and their rhetoric about social security. Tories used the language of work and family to divide, to set people against one another and to obscure realities about where power lay; all absolutely at the polar opposite of what the Labour Party should have been doing.

But Labour's problems on this issue long predate its period in opposition. It was the Social Security Act 2007 – enacted in the final months of Tony Blair's premiership – that laid the roots of the controversial idea that "fitness to work" – and therefore entitlement to benefits – should be decided by Work Capability Assessments conducted by private sector contractors rather than on the basis of medical reports from GPs. Although the assessors were described by the private sector contractors as "health care professionals", they were largely drawn from a range of specialisms which bore little relationship to the conditions that they were expected to assess, based on criteria that were essentially a one-size-fits-all set of questions designed to assess work-related functions rather than the holistic view of an individual's health that a full medical assessment would provide.

The fundamental objection to a functional approach is that it represents a partial and tendentious approach to issues of disability, illness and work in society. It shifts the approach to disability from a social approach – one that emphasises environment and context and sees society's response to disability as the issue to be addressed – to a so-called bio-psychosocial approach that focuses on the individual and their reaction to their environment.

Put briefly, the root of the ideological justification comes from the American sociologist Talcott Parsons' concept of the sick role, which argues that sickness is in essence a form of social deviance, which needs to be policed by medical and other professions. This is associated with the idea that work is essential to well-being (which is true in the sense that those denied the opportunity for meaningful work suffer mental and physical symptoms); so it becomes very easy to move from this to an ideological argument that denying disabled people the ability to live without work is therapeutic (you can also use it to justify the idea of workfare in which benefits are contingent on unpaid work), and of course fits well with populist narratives of workshyness and scrounging. Obviously, he scarcity of meaningful jobs in a long-term economic depression is not considered by this model; it is about the individual, not wider society[10].

Into this environment marched private companies like ATOS and Unum, with experience of developing assessment regimes with a simple aim – that of reducing the number of people on benefits. To do so they can present a ready-made pseudo-scientific model to politicians and advisers in need of a quick result; and you have the current mess. And the pseudo-science closely matches the ideological preconceptions and prejudices of those in power, substituting that for nuanced and complex evidence. It is intellectually and morally simplistic – a form of flatpack policy-making, as it were. And the net effect of this policy is a reversal of a fundamental Labour principle – because, instead of its traditional view that the state owed a duty to the poor, Labour was now accepting implicitly that poor people owed a duty to society.

Unsurprisingly, the Coalition government used this framework as the basis for an extended attack on basis of welfare payments for those who were living with both

---

[10] A fuller - if far from impartial – account of the difference between the social and the bio-psychological model can be found at https://dpac.uk.net/2012/04/a-tale-of-two-models-disabled-people-vs-unum-atos-government-and-disability-charities-debbie-jolly/

physical and mental illness.   In the face of this, the Labour Party – the authors of the system – simply acquiesced.

One of the most notorious examples of Labour collaboration concerned its refusal in 2013 to oppose legislation to re-impose sanctions relating to the Government's work schemes after the High Court had ruled that they were unlawful – the so-called Poundland Case[11]l.

Faced with the appeal court's decision that sanctions had been applied unlawfully the Government's decision was to change the law retrospectively to avoid compensating those who had suffered loss. In other words, those who had been wronged were to be denied their legal recompense. Labour refused to take a stand but abstained on the vote.

The rationale, as set out by Labour's then DWP spokesman Liam Byrne in the House of Commons[12], was instructive and revealing. He deployed two arguments; that sanctions were necessary and should not be undermined, and that the cost of compensation would undermine the public finances.

The second of these arguments is wholly fraudulent: the cost of the compensation would have been a modest £130m – an insignificant sum compared with the DWP budget as a whole, and a small fraction of what the DWP gains through underclaiming of benefits. Moreover, affordability is, in a liberal democracy, no reason for undermining due process.

The first is more significant. It is obvious that Byrne was desperately anxious to retain a system of sanctions in the face of a system in which the DWP has effectively been turned into a gangmaster providing free labour, paid for by the taxpayer, for a number of undertakings including vast – and vastly profitable – supermarket chains.

This in turn reflects the fact that the Labour Party had, both in government and in opposition, been a strong supporter of the idea of workfare – that people should in effect work for their benefits if they were able to do so[13]. The concept of Workfare

[11]   https://www.theguardian.com/society/2013/mar/19/labour-rush-benefit-rebates-poundland

[12] https://publications.parliament.uk/pa/cm201213/cmhansrd/cm130319/debtext/130319-0002.htm#13031966000002

– imported from Clinton's USA – was to prove enormously controversial, with considerable evidence that, leaving aside the ethics, it was economically counter-productive.

From a theoretical view the point is obvious; if employers are able effectively to employ staff for free under work-for-your-benefit schemes, that will bid down real wages. Moreover, if employers are able to recruit staff that they do not have to pay, to replace workers who would need to be paid at least the minimum wage, that amounts effectively to a subsidy to businesses. The effect on people in low-paid, unskilled jobs is therefore *exactly* what its critics claim immigration is doing. And, indeed, there was considerable evidence that this might be happening; research by the Resolution Foundation, showing that real wages started falling at around the time that the stricter application of these schemes by the Coalition was taking place; and other evidence demonstrated that the effect was particularly pronounced in those locations – including some very depressed areas like Merthyr Tydfil in South Wales – where most of the local job opportunities for young people with few qualifications were in the retail sector, which was most likely to be employing staff on workfare schemes.

Sanctions were at the heart of Labour's visions of workfare ever since the Blair government introduced it – even where those concerned have a lifetime of national insurance contributions behind them. The rhetoric is indistinguishable from that of the Victorian Poor Law Guardians, arguing that relief for poverty must be made so undesirable, so humiliating that to seek support should put one beyond the pale of decency; Tory Secretary of State for Work and Pensions Ian Duncan Smith differed from this only in that his rhetoric about "job snobs[14]" was more clumsily explicit. Unpaid supermarket labour became the workhouse of late capitalism, with benefits reduced to a level where the day-to-day decencies of living are unaffordable.

And, too, Labour had actively supported the benefits cap imposed by the Coalition – the rule that there should be a maximum level of benefits available for any one households.

In all of these cases Labour was acquiescing in the ideology that citizenship is not a right, but a condition of what you contribute to the economy. The issue of

---

[13]   https://www.opendemocracy.net/ourkingdom/christopher-barrie/from-welfare-to-workfare-how-helping-hand-became-contract

[14] https://www.telegraph.co.uk/news/politics/9095050/Iain-Duncan-Smith-its-better-to-be-a-shelf-stacker-than-a-job-snob.html

what constitutes citizenship had been becoming increasingly significant in societies where concerns over both immigration and welfare were politically important, and were challenging traditional ideas of universalism. In an article entitled *Post-Fascism* in the Boston Review in 2000 – originally prompted by the rise of Jorg Haider's Freedom Party in Austria – the Hungarian academic G M Tamas[15] gave an account of the implications of this change, describing how the apparent triumph of market capitalism has led to a breakdown of narratives about class and economic power, with the left focusing instead on issues of civil rights and identity; and Tamas, quoting Lipset, describes a "fascism of the centre" in which hostility to the state combines with a belief that rights are not universal, but are the preserve of a particular group, usually based around national or ethnic identity. For the first time in history, popular ire about unfairness in society is being directed not at those wielding wealth and power, but at the dispossessed. In other words, Labour was acquiescing in fundamental changes to conceptions of citizenship and democracy.

Writing in the shadow of total war, and with the slump of the 1930's fresh in his memory, Beveridge saw universal benefits both as more cost-effective – but also as a tool to create social cohesion - a recognition that all had a stake in society, whether rich or poor. Writing in the aftermath of European Fascism and the struggle of total war (a war in which victory was intimately bound-up with the mobilisation of state power) Beveridge was keen to see benefits as a route to stability and an expression of citizenship; all were to have rights, including the right to a basic minimum standard of living.

During the Cameron era the UK, Beveridge's vision was wholly abandoned – in an age of austerity we are told that we simply cannot afford a generous welfare state. Leaving aside the obvious economic question of whether making substantial cuts to the incomes of the poorest in society was a sensible tactic at a time of deep recession, the key point here is that Labour, just as much as the Tories, was complicit in a redefinition of the nature of citizenship, and was clearly abandoning its core values. And ironically, since those in work were affected by cuts, this ideology was – quite obviously – self-defeating on its own terms too. It was in a key sense taking a journey into the darkest heart of neoliberalism[16], insofar as it was

---

[15] http://bostonreview.net/archives/BR25.3/tamas.html

[16] The concept of "neoliberalism" is slippery and hard to define: it has become a standard political insult rather than a term that defines economic and political phenomena with any precision. I have therefore sought, on the whole, to avoid it – even though many adherents of the Corbyn Labour Party will define their own politics as being "against neoliberalism". .

accepting a model of citizenship that was based around participation in a consumerist market economy.

There was one further key issue – one that predated Labour's departure from office but continued to cast the longest of shadows over discourse in the Labour Party: that of the invasion of Iraq. Tony Blair's decision to take part in military intervention in Iraq was exposed by history to have been based on seriously false premises – there were no "weapons of mass destruction" that would have constituted the immediate military threat on which any legal basis for military action would have been based, and there was no evidence whatsoever that the military action in Iraq had made the world safer; indeed, the chaos that the invasion had left behind had crucially undermined the case not just for this particular military invasion but for the idea of liberal interventionism as a whole. It was an intervention that had split and damaged the Labour Party at the time, and became the defining event of what was becoming known as "Blairism".

Subsequent events in the Middle East – where Blair was working as an envoy [insert details] did little to make either the man or his policy more credible. Subsequent issue of military intervention in Syria had exposed the split in Labour – between those who continued to support a form of liberal interventionism and the "anti-Imperialist" wing of the Party who regarded the problems of the Middle East as being essentially the result of Western meddling – with particular blame focused on the United States and the state of Israel.

Major Israeli offensives in Gaza in 2012 and 2014 intensified the anti-Western feeling on the Left – although interestingly the criticism of Israel was often expressed in the language of liberal interventionism; suggesting that we are dealing with different aspects of a the same coin of Western exceptionalism.

Finally, there was deep disillusion with the political system itself. There was a growing belief that the politicians themselves were self-seeking and corrupt, most notably as a result of the Parliamentary expenses scandal. The process of politics itself had become corrupted; politicians and bankers were regarded as being in each other's pockets, and politicians were seen to be remote. Above all, among those involved in politics on the Left and Centre-left, there was a belief that political debate had become confined to an increasingly narrow set of issues, while the big economic issues went by default and were seen to be beyond the scope of political debate – a situation that was widely identified as "neoliberalism".

Faced with this disillusion, the one attempt by mainstream Labour to try and come to terms with these issues was the creation of what has become known as Blue Labour – an attempt to try and reconnect with what was seen as Labour's declining working-class base by creating a political discourse that reflected what were described as traditional working-class values. The problem, however, was two-fold. First, the attempt was made by people – mainly academics and professional politicians – who had little knowledge of working-class communities. Second, and even more damaging, the Blue Labour framing of working-class values was almost entirely in terms of things that were essentially elite constructs – flag, family, nationality – and therefore patronized working-class people rather than enabling them. The fact that something so obviously flawed was the best on offer is a powerful comment on the intellectual poverty of the Labour Right at this time. It emphasized one of the most frequent complaints about New Labour in office – that it chose to direct, from the centre, rather than to listen.

In the circumstances, then, a key issue for the left was how to recapture those five million Labour votes lost since 1997. The argument was that political debate had become a set of ritual exchanges between different flavours of neoliberalism, rather than a forum in which basic questions were being discussed. Some of those five million votes were undoubtedly seduced by the growing appeal of the far Right, towards the UK Independence Party (UKIP) which offered simplistic solutions to deep-seated problems, based around immigration and the EU; but it is not difficult to understand the appeal of the argument that Labour had simply lost touch with the aspirations and needs of millions of its core supporters. In the despair that followed the 2015 General Election, it is not hard to see how that argument could gain so much traction among Labour supporters and members.

In summary, then, there were four key factors that were preparing the ground for a challenge to the social and political programme adopted by Labour in opposition, and which were able to find expression Corbyn's insurgent challenge for the Labour Leadership:

- the politics and economics of austerity and the sense that it was an unnecessary political agenda, nothing to do with economic imperatives; along with Labour's failure to oppose it, and to provide a framing outside austerity; and the fact that such a cautious economic narrative obviously failed in the 2015 election, where Labour's weakness on the economy - its lack of a convincing narrative - had been ruthlessly exposed; and mixed in with this a failure to challenge Tory narratives around social security (it was Labour that created the WCA regime for social security claimants, and used workfare). Also examine how the 2007 crash eliminated the possibility of a Blairite economic approach that used growth to fund growing public expenditure without the need for more progressive taxation.

- A growing sense of a deepening crisis in capitalism and a resurgence in anti-Capitalist narratives; a growing feeling that perhaps Marx was right. At a more prosaic level, the experience of falling real incomes, growing inequalities and in particular in-work poverty, representing the breakdown of the fundamental deal of capitalism, stimulated a feeling that the economic problems were systemic rather than a curable blip in the economic order. The fetishising of work at a time when it was becoming progressively less rewarding for a growing number of people at the bottom of the economic pile.

- A growing resurgence of the nationalist Right - UKIP - also exploiting those economic uncertainties. Labour has been profoundly ambiguous on these issues - immigration and especially the rise of Blue Labour

- A rejection of the Blair government's approach to international affairs, and of the idea of explicit liberal intervention; and, alongside that, a view of world affairs that saw the influence of the US and its allies (In particular Israel) as malign.

What all this appeared to amount to was, in domestic policy, a serious failure of political courage on Labour's part; an unwillingness to challenge the Coalition framing - some of which, on social security in particular, was in any case inherited from Labour. And of course that compounded the doubts that already existed in liberal-left circles over Labour's policy in Iraq, and the general direction that foreign policy in the Middle-East in particular had followed since the Blair years.

In conclusion, then, Labour's performance in the years between 2010 and 2015 displayed a lack of leadership, a lack of imagination, and above all a lack of moral and political courage. It did absolutely nothing to develop its own narrative on the big economic issues, and – despite occasional moments of imagination from Ed Miliband - had offered little in the way of thinking that went beyond a modest amelioration of the worst aspects of Coalition austerity and political framing.

Most of all, it failed to address the fundamental point about Coalition austerity – that it was a political choice. At every stage, the Tories and Liberal Democrats were allowed by an intellectually-exhausted Labour Opposition to get away with the lie that austerity was inevitable. And the Faustian Pact that this was all the price of getting re-elected was blown away in the realities of the 2015 Election defeat – Labour's worst result since they faced Margaret Thatcher in her pomp in 1987, a thrashing of historic proportions[17] for a Labour party expecting at least a share in Government.

And it was against this background that the Labour leadership election of 2015 was held – an election in which the failures of Labour in opposition provided the unavoidable political context.

---

[17] https://www.ft.com/content/263584b0-f4fd-11e4-abb5-00144feab7de

THE 2015 LABOUR LEADERSHIP ELECTION

Against the background of a shattering election defeat, Ed Miliband stood down immediately as Labour leader, with Harriet Harman taking over as interim leader until the election for a successor could be held.

It is not the purpose of this book to give a detailed chronology of the Leadership election of 2015; the events, from Jeremy Corbyn narrowly squeaking on to the nomination sheet to his massive victory a couple of months later, have been extensively chronicled elsewhere. My purpose here is to describe the politics behind that unexpected win, and in particular to examine some of the factors that led to it.

Since Corbyn's victory, a vast amount has been written about the reasons why this unexpected victory should have happened. Perhaps the best way to explain it is a combination of political and organisational circumstances which enabled Corbyn to capitalise on the political situation I described in the previous chapter.

In the aftermath of the election, a number of theories were proposed as to why Corbyn had won. These, according to the author of a book on Corbyn published after his win, included[18]:

- It was Ed Miliband's fault for changing the voting system.
- It was the fault of MPs who nominated him despite not wanting him to be leader.
- Harriet Harman made a strategic mistake in forcing the shadow cabinet to abstain over welfare cuts.

---

[18]

http://eprints.lse.ac.uk/79178/1/LSE%20Government%20%E2%80%93%20How%20did%20social%20media%20help%20Corbyn%20win%20the%20Labour%20leadership_.pdf

- Andy Burnham was to blame, for pandering to the Left.
- Yvette Cooper should have stood aside for Burnham.
- It was Tony Blair's fault. It was Iraq; it was New Labour; it was the expenses scandal; it was the global rise of anti-austerity movements.

All of these may have played their parts – and, in the aftermath of the election, some of them may have been exaggerated.

The first of these is a common complaint; that the widening of the franchise in the election meant that the process was skewed by the inclusion of those who were able to register for £3 as party "supporters"; a process that some claimed led to mass entryism by people who were not really Labour supporters at all. But this claim is not borne out by the facts of the vote. The results[19] show that Corbyn had a clear lead among all three categories of vote – members, registered supporters and affiliates (Political levy-paying Trade Unionists and members of bodies formally affiliated to the Labour Party). It's true that the registered supporters were the largest group, and it is here that Corbyn achieved his biggest vote – but among members he won a whisker less than 50% of the first preference vote. A members' only vote would have seen him comfortably elected, as it seems reasonable to expect that not all the votes of the other candidates would have transferred to each other.

Results 1st Stage	Members	Registered Supporters	Affiliated Supporters	Total	% of Valid Vote
BURNHAM, Andy	55,698	6,160	18,604	80,462	19.0%
COOPER, Yvette	54,470	8,415	9,043	71,928	17.0%
CORBYN, Jeremy	121,751	88,449	41,217	**251,417**	59.5%
KENDALL, Liz	13,601	2,574	2,682	18,857	4.5%
TOTAL	245,520	105,598	71,546	422,664	

Source: Labour Party

---

[19]

https://web.archive.org/web/20160721231632/http://www.labour.org.uk/blog/entry/results-of-the-labour-leadership-and-deputy-leadership-election

Indeed, such attempts at entryism as were detected by the Labour Party's compliance team came from rather different sources. There were persistent media stories of Tories attempting to register as supporters to vote for Corbyn[20], and, more curiously, it was reported that more than 3000 Green Party members had been caught attempting to register to vote in the election – which is considerably more than voted in the Greens' own most recent leadership election, even if one discounts those who got through the net[21].

What one might define as the "hard left" in the UK – both within the Labour party and outside it – probably amounted to no more than a few thousand people around the country. There is no doubt that some of those who had been involved in Left politics in the past took part – many either through rejoining Labour or becoming registered supporters. Professor Colin Talbot of Cambridge University estimates that perhaps the non-Labour left amounted to 50,000 people at its 1970-80s peak – although he suggested that the rapid churn of members may mean that there are hundreds of thousands of former members. Some of course will have simply drifted away from politics[22]. Talbot writes[23]:

> "Few of the 'ex-comrades', I would suggest, ever really settled intellectual accounts with their 'revolutionary socialist' flings. They voted overwhelmingly for Blair in '97 and tolerated the 'Third Way', to the extent they thought about it at all between school-runs, but not enthusiastically.
>
> It is this mass of vaguely 'socialist' middle-aged ex-Trots – and there are an awful lot more of them than they or anyone else probably realized until recently – that might explain a lot of the 'Corbyn' phenomena. Disillusioned with Blair (mainly over one single issue – Iraq), despondent of Labour ever winning again anyway, they have turned to Corbyn as the political equivalent of going out and buying a Harley."

---

[20]   https://www.theguardian.com/politics/2015/aug/18/tory-party-member-votes-for-jeremy-corbyn-three-times

[21] As tweeted by Faisal Islam in August 2015

[22] A source who was active in Militant as a student in the 1980s recalls one fervent expounder of the faith whose fervour evaporated on being offered a graduate traineeship at city accountants Arthur Andersen.

[23]   https://colinrtalbot.wordpress.com/2016/07/26/corbynism-not-turning-labour-into-a-socialist-movement-but-turning-a-socialist-movement-into-labour/

Talbot undoubtedly describes a real phenomenon, but there is little real evidence to suggest that – whatever may have happened since - entryism played a major role in the Corbyn victory.

The second point – about MPs who nominated Corbyn without really wanting him to win – seems weak. It begs the obvious question about what would have happened to the Labour Party if there had not been a challenge from outside the consensus; whatever one's view of the failures or successes of Corbynism, it seems that without some profound shock there would have been nothing on offer but more of what had lost Labour the 2015 election. One might characterise the choice in 2015 as one between a heroic leap into the unknown and a comfortable but inevitable decline. It is not necessary to be a Corbynist to understand that Labour could not go on as it was in 2015. Something had to give.

On the third point, there can be little doubt that the decision of interim leader Harriet Harman not to oppose further welfare cuts was a lightning rod that allowed the discharge of real anger about Labour's direction.

Barely a month after the election defeat, Harriet Harman announced that the Labour Party would not vote against Government proposals in a Welfare Bill that, among other things, imposed a cap on child benefit for the first two children. It was a decision that caused a furore, with 48 Labour MPs eventually breaking the Labour whip to vote against the measure[24].

Harman's rationale is interesting. Labour, she argued, had suffered two election defeats; they could not oppose the expressed will of the people[25]. It was, yet again, the argument from electability rather than on the basis of what was right or wrong; Labour's problems in opposition encapsulated. Although all four of the Labour leadership candidates had criticised the move, only one – Jeremy Corbyn, a serial rebel whose dissent would have surprised nobody – voted in defiance of the whip[26]. As well as acting as a focus for anger about Labour's direction, it allowed Corbyn to present himself as the principled candidate in the debate.

---

[24] https://www.theguardian.com/politics/2015/jul/12/harman-labour-not-vote-against-welfare-bill-limit-child-tax-credits

[25] Thus, ironically, anticipating Corbyn's position on Brexit – see Chapter 7 below

[26] https://www.theguardian.com/politics/2015/jul/21/labour-disarray-welfare-48-mps-defy-whips

Moreover, a second rationale – used by those on the Labour Right to defend the decision – was that this was only a second reading debate; it did not therefore commit Labour to the measure. Ironically, this was exactly the rationale used by defenders of the Labour leadership's decision to whip in support of the Brexit legislation less than three years later; on both occasions it looks like excuse-mongering and special pleading.

The fourth point at least introduces the performances of the other candidates into the debate. Politically, it is important to understand the dynamic of the other three candidates – Andy Burnham, Yvette Cooper and Liz Kendall – and how the similarities of their platforms (some might say the similarities of their evasions) created a situation in which there was a clear divide between them and the Corbyn campaign.

And what this meant was that in the leadership election, there were three candidates who were on the "moderate" wing of the Labour Party, who implicitly accepted the Tory framing around these issues, and were happy to develop their policy positions on the same assumptions as the coalition. In doing so, they were accepting a prescription that Ed Miliband's leadership had been "too left wing" – whereas in fact, the Miliband years had seen a shift to the Right – both in terms of the rhetoric and, on economics, in the fact of the policy. As Shadow Chancellor, Ed Balls had explicitly repudiated the policies that his mentor, Gordon Brown, enacted both as Chancellor and Prime Minister; most of all in the period immediately following the crash of 2007-8, when the then Labour Government used fiscal expansion alongside the recapitalisation of the banks to ensure that the economy recovered; but also the use of public expenditure to allow investment, especially in schools and hospitals, that partly offset the failure of the private sector to invest during the same period. The problem was not that Ed Balls – and the three mainstream leadership candidates in 2015 – were Blairites; it was that, on economic policy, and on welfare, and immigration, they had moved significantly to the Right of Blair's positions on domestic issues, at a time when the effects of the 2007 crash demanded that a fundamentally different economic approach was needed. There was never, in the language and presentation of mainstream Labour economic policy, any sense that austerity was a political *choice*. And in that point Labour was in effect siding with the Government, and not providing any real opposition at all.

And, following a General Election in which Labour's biggest weakness was its failure to convince the electorate on economic policy, it was obvious that Balls' reluctance to challenge the Tories' framing had achieved less than nothing; Labour had actually slipped back, rather than delivering the advances that many Labour people expected the Party to make. Despite the longest sustained fall in living standards since the 1870s, and the Coalition austerity policies that were both cause and effect of that fall, Labour had lost the argument.

And in that context, it becomes clear that Jeremy Corbyn became identified, not with a hard-left programme, but with a political stance that spoke directly to the natural instincts of the great majority of Labour Party members: opposition to austerity; decent welfare provision (and instinctive opposition to the Tories' 2015 proposals to cut benefits further, on which, as we have seen, the Parliamentary leadership had ordered MPs to abstain); a liberal view on immigration. Corbyn, like the majority of Labour MPs at the time, voted against the Iraq War; on what many Labour members regarded as the most shameful episode of Labour's time in office, he was on their side.

One of the keys to understanding the Labour Party – something that people outside it don't always understand – is the emotional bond that keeps the Party together. During my own time in Labour Politics I have heard innumerable references to the Labour "family" - although as a party we have our internal differences, and we have our divisions and rows, ultimately as Labour Party members we are bound by something very deep that we hold in common.

The fact is that Labour people are usually idealists – even the most hardened political campaigners are people brought into the Labour movement by ideals and beliefs. They continue to be true believers, even as they continue to be pragmatists, and the fantasy that a left-wing leader steeped in their values could be swept into power on a Socialist platform is the pay-off for all the meetings, all that canvassing and leafletting in the pouring rain, the moments of despair, the interminable frustrations. For even the most battle-hardened pragmatists, these things matter. One of the standard texts, as it were, for the Labour faithful is the opening scene of the TV adaptation of Chris Mullin's A Very British Coup, in which we see newly elected Socialist Prime Minister Harry Perkins' triumphant arrival in Downing Street. "Do you want to abolish first class?" says a journalist to Perkins as he travels South to London from his Northern constituency. "No, I want to abolish second class" Perkins replies[27]. It's a moment whose emotional appeal is absolutely authentic and goes straight to the heart of anyone who has given their time and effort to the Labour movement, and still remembers why they do it. After nearly two decades in which Labour had been told that the head must lead the heart – one of

---

[27] https://www.youtube.com/watch?v=vgI9hjRzmq0

the inevitable consequences of being in government after 1997, but then reinforced in opposition when people across the Party were being asked to acquiesce in the name of electability in things they found profoundly unsettling and distasteful – Corbyn, especially as the momentum gathered and the rallies filled – gave them – us – licence to dream again.

And, above all, when Labour had suffered a traumatic election defeat, it seemed clear that the evasions of Ed Balls' economic policy were no longer valid. The message that Labour needed to be "responsible" in its economic policy no longer worked – every Labour member who had been on the doorstep in the 2015 campaign knew that Labour wasn't trusted on economic policy. Polls showed that Labour was ahead on every other issue, but Labour had abandoned its instinct on the economy and it simply hadn't worked. But the catastrophe of austerity economics was clear for everyone to see; and Labour was not challenging it. It was a false position and electors knew it.

And the crucial point that Corbyn's opponents missed was that the world had moved on since 1997 – the crash of 2008 had meant that New Labour's basic economic model – that of using strong growth to generate the funds to allow higher spending on public services, while running a modest deficit to pay for public sector investment (and hence covering for the private sector's investment strike) was no longer deliverable or appropriate. Specifically, during the austerity period the fundamental economic conditions – low interest rates (greatly reducing the cost of public borrowing), falling real incomes (and therefore demand), a continuing productivity crisis and the emergence of theories of secular stagnation, in which full employment can only be maintained by overheating economies – were entirely different from those of the Blair and Brown years.

In other words, Jeremy Corbyn's appeal was not that he was left-wing, or that the causes that he had promoted from the back-benches were popular. It was, quite simply, that he was the only candidate who spoke to Labour mainstream – who appeared capable of articulating values that reminded people what Labour was for and who it existed to serve. And he spoke to Labour's heart, rather than its head. It was something that no Labour leader had done for some time.

Most of all, it is vital to understand that Corbyn's appeal had nothing to do with entryism. Entryism a tactic that has been used by the Trotskyite Left over many decades, aiming to move mainstream parties towards a programme of "transitional demands"; the aim is that mainstream social democratic parties should be set up to fail to deliver those programmes, with the aim of increasing the credibility of the revolutionary vanguard movement that is dedicated to delivering a genuine Socialist programme. There is no doubt that the unexpected success of the Corbyn campaign, and the system of registered supporters, provided the opportunity for entryism; Michael Crick, author of the standard work on the Trotskyist Militant Tendency[28], remarked in the introduction to the latest edition of the book that, covering the Corbyn campaign, he saw a good number of familiar faces in the queues outside Corbyn meetings[29]. But it's also true that, despite having been a familiar figure on the Left over decades, and having opposed the expulsion of Militant during the 1980s, Corbyn was never close to any of the factions outside the Labour Party - least of all those like Militant and the Socialist Workers' Party that, in their very different ways, were Trotskyite in ideology.

However, both during the election campaign and since, Corbyn has received widespread support from those on the left outside the Labour Party, and his victory has undoubtedly brought some of those on the non-Labour left back into the Party – a fact that has, for example, led Momentum to change its rules to ensure that all those holding office in that organisation must be Labour members (which means, under Labour Party rules, that they must not be members of any other Party that stands or has stood candidates against Labour). But that is not the same as saying that Corbyn's win was down to entryism.

So far we have considered the negative reasons for backing Corbyn – examining what Jeremy Corbyn wasn't. What, then, was the positive appeal of Corbyn to the thousands of people – Labour members and supporters – who elected him so emphatically?

During the 2015 Labour leadership campaign, a piece appeared in the Independent newspaper, written by a student named Lucas Fothergill[30]. He listed a number of reasons why he – and others like him – were supporting Corbyn's leadership bid. In summary:

---

[28] Crick *Militant* (2016 edn),]

[29] At the meeting I attended in Cardiff during the election campaign, the row in front of where I was sitting was deftly and expertly commandeered by the Swansea SWP, in a display of collective discipline of which Trotsky himself might have approved.

[30] https://www.independent.co.uk/student/istudents/labour-leadership-race-2015-im-a-student-and-this-is-why-ill-be-voting-for-jeremy-corbyn-10459461.html

- People argued that Corbyn was "unelectable". But in 2015 Labour had been led by people who stressed "electability" and had still lost;
- Labour under Corbyn would be differentiated from the Conservative Party, offering something new rather than more of the same;
- Corbyn is principled and people connect with him
- Corbyn has opposed personal attacks and doesn't smear his opponents
- Corbyn's policy positions resonate with young people
- Corbyn had the lowest expenses claim of any MP

We will return to the extent to which these claims have been borne out by subsequent events, but the principal elements of the Corbyn narrative are all there (and one notes in passing that of those six points, only the second relates directly to his political position). Above all, Corbyn is presented as an insurgent – as someone who has pursued a solitary and principled line over decades, while all around him have sold out the core values of the Labour Party; the point about the expenses claim is particularly important when there is little that did more to undermine public faith in mainstream Westminster politics than the revelations that MPs were routinely increasing their expenses entitlement by swapping homes, employing family members and – in one notorious case – expecting the taxpayer to stump up the costs of cleaning out their moat[5].

There is little doubt that Corbyn is seen as a different kind of politician, promoting a new kind of politics. Such an approach was bound to have a strong appeal in 2015, when conventional Parliamentary politics was seen to be in deep crisis. But much the same could have been said of Tony Blair before 1997, or even of David Cameron in his "hug a hoodie" phase; indeed, every political leader in recent years – with the possible exception of Theresa May – has tried to claim they offered a new style of politics. What makes Corbyn different?

The issue of insurgency is a common one among populist politicians. One thing that Corbyn has in common with politicians on what might be termed the insurgent fringe – Nigel Farage, Caroline Lucas - is the claim of being outside the political mainstream; of being a different kind of politician. All are compared with the political mainstream and represent themselves as "anti-establishment", as outsiders to the political process.

It is true that none of them has followed the mainstream Westminster political career path, and Corbyn is the only one of the three who belongs to a mainstream political party. But the claim that they are somehow outside the political establishment is nonsense. They all come from privileged backgrounds – fitting precisely the social and demographic model of those who enter professional politics - and have all been professional politicians for decades. And none have held the kind of political office that brings with it the need to make – and subsequently defend – difficult political decisions. All governmental decisions involve trade-offs and conflicts, at any level; It is very easy to present oneself as somehow politically "pure" when one has never engaged in the need to deal with those kinds of conflicts. The essence of populism is simplification, which allows politicians to make sweeping moral statements on the basis of partial understandings of the facts of a decision.

And, at a time when for various reasons, mainstream Westminster politics is in disrepute, it becomes relatively easy for that kind of populism to take hold. But at the same time it is a form of political disengagement – and it certainly isn't the politics of the Left. It represents a failure, at one level, to understand what the politics of liberal democracy is; that it is almost always messy, involving trade-offs and compromises. Making political decisions is not easy, and to pretend otherwise is to indulge in the sort of simplification that is at the heart of populist authoritarianism.

<u>Corbyn and social media</u>

It is a commonplace that the 2015 Labour leadership election was the first in which social media played a significant role. Indeed, social media has been claimed to have played a major role in bringing about Corbyn's decision to stand at all.

A survey by Yougov[31] of the electorate in the Leadership election showed, among other things, that Corbyn's supporters were far more likely than those of his opponents to get their news principally from social media.   The influence of social media on the politics of Corbynism are discussed more fully in Chapter 5 below, but it's worth reflecting on a few general points.

The most obvious one is that the level of commitment needed to be part of a social media event is low – it takes minimal effort to click on a link, or to "like" a Facebook post or to retweet. However, at a time when it is generally believed that active political participation has fallen – and in which the politics of the mainstream parties appears to have become more remote from the public – such activity can acquire the appearance of authenticity; it can look like the voice of the people.

---

[31]   https://yougov.co.uk/news/2015/08/27/you-may-say-im-dreamer-inside-mindset-jeremy-corby/

In practice, this can mean that social media can play an important role in gathering support behind an idea – or a candidate – and giving the appearance, whether legitimate or not, of public support. It means that the number of clicks or likes can very easily become a surrogate for public support.[32]

It became very clear during the 2015 leadership election that Corbyn's team, far more than his opponents, was able to use social media, including events such as Twitterstorms, to generate momentum behind their candidate. This partly represents the fact that they were working with a demographic – young, professional and generally affluent – that was comfortable with the use of social media. While his opponents had a social media presence they used it far less adroitly.

And, as was argued at the time, Corbyn the man was a perfect subject for a social media campaign, because he was different. He had idiosyncracies that made him immediately different from his competitors, and instantly recognized; he had eccentricities of manner, dress and behaviour that set him apart from three, frankly, identikit politicians. All of this made him the perfect figure to become an internet sensation[33]; and helped cement the idea that he was offering something new, exciting and different.

How did Corbyn's opponents react?

It is abundantly clear that Corbyn's opponents in the leadership election had no idea of how to deal with the insurgency. They remained locked inside a their own political and economic bubble.

Nothing perhaps illustrates this better than their competition to adopt the idea of "aspiration" as their own. Candidates claimed that Labour under Ed Miliband failed to understand or encourage it, and if Labour is to win again it must embrace it.

As commonly understood, aspiration is about the will of individuals to "get on", to achieve a decent and rising standard of living for themselves (and their families).

---

[32] This thesis is set out in more detail – in the context of Brexit – at https://www.diggitmagazine.com/papers/brexit-and-online-political-activism

[33] https://www.theguardian.com/politics/2015/aug/04/jezwecan-jeremy-corbyn-social-media-vote-labour-leadership

It was a message that chimed well with the "hard working families" rhetoric that was commonplace across the political spectrum.

However, in the political and economic circumstances of 2015 – characterised by almost zero growth, falling real living standards and – in particular – the crisis in productivity that no mainstream politicians appeared willing to talk about, the idea of aspiration was far from progressive. In a world of zero productivity growth, real incomes can increase in one of three ways: through movement into work, through benign falls in commodity prices (which of course can have catastrophic effects on primary producers) or, crucially, if one person's income rises at the expense of another's: aspiration at a time of flat productivity is, other things being equal, a zero sum game.

What it means in political terms is that "aspiration" - in the terms expressed by Corbyn's opponents - is the enemy of equality. One prominent Corbyn supporter, Jon Trickett MP, argued that the emphasis on aspiration was in essence a coded way of saying that inequality was acceptable; and identified this as one of a number of factors that showed that the Labour Party had lost its way[34]. And, ultimately, Trickett's comment was really an expression of cold economic fact – that unless the economy is expanding and productivity is growing, promoting individual aspiration in these terms is a *cause* of inequality. And the reality, in 2015, was that real incomes had fallen at a rate unprecedented for much more than a century, and the lower the income, the faster the fall. For many at the bottom end of the income scale – especially those dependent on social security (which obviously included millions of people in work) – the issue was not one of aspiration, but of simple survival. And these are the people who, it has long been argued on the Labour left, deserted Labour in droves in 2010, and stayed away in 2015.

But aspiration, as described by what one might call the continuity candidates in 2015, was also politically as well as economically problematic. It had become fashionable to discount the post-war social democratic settlement, but that provided the basis on which aspiration was benign and a driver of positive change – investment, productivity growth, a steady rise in real incomes for the majority. And many of the things that fall under the umbrella of aspiration were delivered *collectively* – better health care, education, decent housing.

---

34 https://labourlist.org/2015/05/jon-trickett-says-labours-policies-didnt-lose-them-election-and-criticises-leadership-candidates/

By the same token, there has been no more socially destructive policy than the sale of council houses – which remains the touchstone of aspiration for the right. Thirty five years on, it remains a root cause of a profound and unprecedented housing crisis. And in 2015 the Tories justify the extension of right-to-buy to housing association stock in the name of aspiration. In other words to the extent that Labour people were talking about individual aspiration, they were essentially accepting – here as elsewhere – an explicitly Conservative framing.

In other words, the big idea among the other candidates was a damp squib. And it fundamentally misjudged the mood of the party; they were seen as part of the old Labour consensus, one that had demonstrably failed in 2015, and had absolutely nothing to offer in response to the emotional surge that occurred; the Labour of managerialism, of young men in suits with laptops, had nothing to offer in response to Corbyn's old time revivalism. Contemporary reports paint a picture of campaign staffers sitting shellshocked in coffee shops and bars, completely shellshocked by the Corbyn surge, without the vocabulary or the experience to understand what had been unleashed on them.

In summary, then, Corbyn offered a range of attributes that set him apart from his competitors. He offered the hope of a clean break from a dismal past; he was a candidate uniquely suited to the dynamics of social media; he was able to make an appeal to the visceral heart of a Labour traumatized by election defeat. But, most of all, he appeared to offer a decisive break from a politics that had failed – electorally, politically, ideologically.

And, a year later, when he faced a challenge from Owen Smith for the leadership, he was still able to mobilise on that basis – although in one sense a large part of the battle had been won. In terms of political and economic agenda, Smith presented himself as a powerful opponent of austerity, who argued at hustings meetings that he shared much of Corbyn's economic and social analysis; he presented himself not as the candidate who had an alternative political agenda, but as the candidate who could win[35]. Blairism was dead; a year on from Corbyn's first victory the debate was tactical, not ideological.

---

[35]   https://notesbrokensociety.wordpress.com/2016/08/05/labours-cardiff-hustings-a-view-from-the-hall/

LABOUR, LENINISM AND MOMENTUM

In September 2015, the new Labour leader was an unknown quantity – having come from nowhere in a matter of a few months. Going beyond the policy positions, what was Corbyn's political heritage and method?

With Corbyn's Labour drawing in many groups and individuals from Left groups outside the Labour Party it's important to consider whether Corbyn's Labour has moved away from the model of the party established by the 1918 constitution to something altogether different. Although, as discussed above, Corbyn's victory is not a matter of Leftist entryism, there is little doubt that figures from the more traditional organised Left – both inside and outside the Labour Party – have played a significant role in the development of Corbyn's leadership. It is no exaggeration that the general staff of Corbynism represents a coalition of forces across the traditional left, and the phenomenon of Corbynism has brought together a number of strands across a traditionally fissiparous British Left, in which questions of tactics and method have been as influential – and as divisive – as those of ideology.

<u>The origins of Labour</u>

The roots of the modern Labour Party lie in the constitution it adopted in 1918, which made a clear commitment to a Parliamentary route to power. Clause 1 of that Constitution establishes the maintenance of a Parliamentary Party as Labour's first objective. That Constitution reflected the first attempt to create Labour as a mass party – for example, for the first time it was possible for individuals to become members, rather than the Party being a federation of affiliated organisations – reflecting the emergence of mass democracy in which all men and, for the first time, some women were entitled to vote. It also represented an uneasy organisational compromise, balancing the need to keep the Trade Unions – as Labour's principal funders – on board while meeting the ideological concerns of the Independent Labour Party, which represented the grass-roots organisations, to a sufficient degree to keep them inside the Party (for now). The resulting compromise was expressed in Clause 4, but the Labour Party that emerged was Parliamentary, Fabian (rooted in the "inevitability of gradualness") and non-revolutionary[36].

The result was a Labour Party that, while explicitly non-Marxist and committed to Parliamentary activity, was able to encompass a broad spectrum of opinion – a Broad Church, as the Party has long liked to describe itself.   Labour's Parliamentarianism has long been criticised on the Left – most notably in Ralph Miliband's classic *Parliamentary Socialism*[37], which argues that this Parliamentarianism has meant that Labour has become a reformist political party, unable to break the bounds of capitalism and with no serious intention of moving beyond that framework; in Miliband's view this was an opportunity lost.

Moreover, it has been widely argued on the classic Marxist left that Labour's problems were less due to its Parliamentarism than to its close links with the Trade Unions. It is a commonplace that the Labour Party was originally established to provide representation for working men in Parliament – a position that, as we have seen, the 1918 Constitution and the adoption of Clause IV in particular, moved some way away from. At a theoretical level, it located its drive for power in the state, itself a capitalist institution. But an alternative view – articulated notably by the late Tony Cliff, a key ideologist of the Socialist Workers Party – argues that the failing of the Labour Party lay less in its Parliamentarism than in its Trade Union-based organisation: that, theoretically in a capitalist democracy, Trade Unions were an ameliorative rather than a revolutionary force, concerned with ensuring the best deal for their members within the capitalist system rather than overthrowing it[38].

And Stuart Hall formulated what he called the contradiction within social democracy[39] – arguing that in opposition a social democratic party spoke up for those people it represented, working-class people and the dispossessed, but in office became the representative of the state; it disciplines, rather than represents, the working class movement (which, in the context of the Labour Party, meant the Trade

---

[36]   http://labour-uncut.co.uk/2013/02/21/labour-history-uncut-labour%E2%80%99s-first-clause-four-moment/

[37] Miliband, Ralph *Parliamentary Socialism* (2009 edn)

[38] http://isj.org.uk/labourism-and-socialism-ralph-milibands-marxism/

[39] In his essay The Great Moving Right Show, published in Marxism Today, January 1979 http://banmarchive.org.uk/collections/mt/pdf/79_01_hall.pdf

Union movement). Writing in 1979, with the Callaghan government's incomes policies fresh in Hall's mind, it is not difficult to see the force of that argument.

However, within the Labour Party mainstream the "broad church" has usually been regarded as a strength; it has been believed that a demonstrably politically diverse Labour Party has had a wider electoral appeal, although at the same time the Labour Party's organisational core has been keen to limit the influence of the more radical Left. Moreover, the Labour Party has always sought to embrace wider progressive political causes; for example some of the more lasting achievements of the Wilson governments of the 1960s were in social reform, including the legalization of abortion and the decriminalization of homosexuality.

One of the implications of Labour's explicit adoption of a Parliamentary programme is that it accepts the constitutional position of Members of Parliament – that their duty to represent extends to all their constituents, not just those who are members of the Labour Party. It is an acceptance of the constitutional principle that has long lain at the heart of representative politics in Britain, since being articulated by Edmund Burke; that Members of Parliament are representatives, not delegates. Indeed the whole concept of Parliamentary Privilege – one of the fundamental principles on which the British model of Parliamentary representation stands – is that Members should be able to use their consciences in what they regard as the best interests of their constituents. Obviously the Party system involves a system of Parliamentary whipping, but the principle remains that the Member of Parliament is answerable to their electorate as a whole, not one small faction within it. But that principle has obviously been contested; the relationship between the elected representative, their party and their constituency has been a key point of issue in Labour's internal debate.

Over decades, organisations on the Trotskyist Left have, at various times, pursued a policy of entryism[40] – of seeking to gain power and influence in the Labour Party in order to pursue their aim, not of getting into government, but of pressing what are called "transitional demands" - more radical policy positions designed to rally public support but which a Labour government, in the tradition of social democratic parties, will be unable to deliver, with the aim of using that failure to mobilise the working class for revolutionary change. The most notable of these periodic attempts at entryism was the rise of Militant in the 1980s, which led to numerous expulsions (Militant lives on as the Socialist Party[41]). At the root of this

---

[40] See Crick, Michael Militant for a detailed history

[41] https://www.socialistparty.org.uk/

strategy has been their argument that Labour, as a social democratic party, is reformist rather than socialist, and as such was an organization that would delay, rather than hasten, the creation of a Socialist society.

One fundamental factor in the development of the Party is that the core ideological group at the heart of Corbyn's Labour Party is drawn from outside the old mainstream. It is instructive to look at the backgrounds of many of Corbyn's closest associates, and the people who assumed important roles in the Corbyn team after his election to the leadership. Most of Corbyn's original team were drawn from the Labour Representation Committee[42], a socialist organization formerly chaired by John McDonnell that drew its members both from within the Labour Party and from Left groups outside the Party (including the Green Party). Key figures from the LRC who formed part of Corbyn's team include Marsha Jane Thompson, his social media adviser, and Andrew Fisher, who advised Corbyn on policy.

As Daniel Allingham points out[43], the usual term of abuse on the centre and right about Corbyn's supporters – "trots" – is wholly inappropriate; Corbyn's immediate circle tends, not towards Trotskyism but towards a much more orthodox Marxist-Leninism. Corbyn himself was a regular columnist in the Morning Star, the Communist Party of Great Britain's newspapers; his close advisers Seamus Milne and Andrew Murray were members of the Communist Party, and both have, at one time or another, pushed an orthodox neo-Stalinist line (although Murray's route to the Leader's office was through the Stop the War Coalition, at one point in its history chaired by Corbyn, and an organisation widely regarded as being a front for the explicitly Trotskyite Socialist Workers' Party). While Corbyn was one of those who argued against the expulsion of the avowedly Trotskyite Militant Tendency from the Labour Party in the 1980s, he was never associated with them.

A Leninist model?

One of the accusations explicitly levelled at Corbyn's Labour Party – for example by Observer and Spectator columnist Nick Cohen[44], but also by some people who were active in the Left in the 1980s - is that it follows a Leninist model of party organisation.

---

[42] https://labourrep.com/

[43]   https://www.newstatesman.com/politics/june2017/2017/04/jeremy-corbyn-has-attracted-socialism-fans-not-labour-voters

[44] See, for example https://blogs.spectator.co.uk/2016/12/marxist-leninists-now-labour-partys-moderates/ -

The Leninist model of party organisation is loosely based on Lenin's 1902 book *What is to be done?*. While interpretations of Lenin's writing obviously vary[45], the main elements of Lenin's model are:

- That the party should consist mainly of intellectuals, on the basis that the workers are not able to organise themselves. This concept derives from the writings of Kautsky but originally appears in *The Communist Manifesto* of 1848, in which Marx and Engels describe the idea of a "vanguard party". The crux of *What is to be done?* Is the argument that workers will not become political simply by fighting battles over pay, working conditions and the like; that they must be led by a vanguard of dedicated intellectuals who could ensure that workers were educated beyond their immediate concerns, to gain a broader understanding of social and political forces.

- The party should be directed by a core of "professional revolutionaries". This did not mean salaried functionaries, but a group of qualified intellectuals who could devote a degree of time and energy to the movement that was beyond the resources of ordinary workers. The implication – even if Lenin did not say so explicitly – was that these people should be intellectuals; the nature of the work demanded as such.

- There should be no place within the movement for spontaneity: there was a need for educated organisation and, in particular, Lenin had no time for anarchism, regarding "spontaneity" as a doctrine that would lead to the defeat of the revolutionary movement. However, the vanguard party should be ready to take advantage of spontaneous political activity and impose its disciplines on such activity.

- That the organisation of the party should be directed from the centre, with the votes of the broad membership endorsing and rationalising the directions of the central command, rather than the grass roots being the place where ideas and political initiatives originated. The rationale for this is the need for the party to represent the class struggle, and not to be

---

[45] A piece that both describes the Leninist model in detail and argues that the usual description is a vulgarised misreading of what Lenin actually wrote can be found at https://www.marxists.org/archive/draper/1990/myth/myth.htm

seduced into the byways of what Lenin would have called "sectism" – small groups based around specific ideas or programmes. The implication of this is that, while unity is important, and there is no virtue in splitting into sects, where the revolutionary wing of a party wins control, it should not make concessions to its opponents for the sake of unity. There is no question of building a broad church party; such a party is deeply inimical to the Leninist model.

What is the evidence that the Labour Party under Corbyn is democratic centralist in spirit and practise?

- The obsession with consolidating power within the party structure, to the exclusion of other issues. One obvious manifestation of this is the obsession with deselection of Labour Party candidates at both Parliamentary and local government level, to be replaced by people who can be trusted to be "socialists". While this phenomenon is most often discussed in Parliamentary terms, it is in local government that some of the most strenuous efforts have been made. In Brighton and Hove, for example, a district where the Labour Party has been largely taken over by Momentum activists (many of whom were, before 2015, members, activists and supporters of the Green Party – while some of whom are currently under suspension from the Party) the Left has devoted much effort in ensuring the election of suitably "socialist" candidates in order to elect the first "socialist" Council in the city's history. This process has been combined with the systematic undermining of the existing minority Labour administration.[46]

- A further example can be drawn for the experience of the Labour Party in Wales, where Momentum's Welsh affiliate, Welsh Labour Grassroots (WLG), has devoted its energies entirely to the issue of securing changes to the system for electing the Leader of Welsh Labour – and, in the current political situation, the First Minister of Wales. In a nation that has borne the brunt of austerity, contains some of the poorest regions in Europe, and whose economic structure leaves it exposed to damage from Brexit to a

---

[46] The process has been closely co-ordinated by Momentum, to the point where identical statements have apparently been circulated for the faithful to read out at their selection meetings. As one local wag put it, it is only a matter of time until Insert Name Here is elected to fight a Council seat.

greater extent than almost any other part of the United Kingdom, the leadership of the Left in Wales has eschewed campaigning on any of these issues in order to work to bring the method for electing the Welsh Labour leader in line with that obtaining in England, and to undermining the Welsh Labour Government, and the current First Minister, who has engaged with those issues and has to a considerable extent mitigated the worst effects of austerity in Wales. The point here is that what might look like a particularly frivolous form of student politics to an outsider is wholly in line with the Leninist view that party structures are more significant than ameliorative policies.

- The structures of Momentum and the far left; the way in which political initiative is controlled at the centre. The rhetoric of the Corbynist party is about being member-led, and that Party structures should be open and democratic. Again, the example of Welsh Labour Grassroots is instructive here; a set of draft standing orders for the organization of WLG/Momentum issued in September 2016[47]. These – which prompted acquaintances of mine who were involved in Militant in the 1980s to comment on the similarity to the rules that obtained in that organization – make it clear that all political initiative lies with the centre; that local groups are not allowed to retain funds for campaigning or to make any meaningful political decisions on their own activities, and must defer to the centre.

- The rhetoric of "centrism" and the demonisation of the "Blairites" - which actually means anyone who is not inside the Momentum/Corbynist tent. The fact is that "Blairite" is the most powerful insult in the Corbynist lexicon, far more than "Tory". The rhetoric of Corbynism is based entirely around simplification and false binaries; if you are pro-Corbyn, you are inside the tent. If you show any inclination to question, or even argue that political life really isn't that simple, you are outside, and not only hostile but willfully so. Your motives are as suspect as your judgement, and you are a "centrist" or "Blairite" and therefore an enemy

- The emergent hostility to Trade Unions – for example, in the campaign by Momentum in to eliminate the Trade Union vote in choosing the Welsh

---

[47]   The   documents   can   be   read   at
https://drive.google.com/open?id=1ZYhBwj_iVD2luRuGPDq0-ZKnoJANpawA   and
https://drive.google.com/open?id=1g8F0J7aEZeIDx1K-9O6FBvpfbC6He6j2

Labour leader; and comments by prominent Momentum and former Labour National Executive member Christine Shawcroft to the effect that the Union link was outmoded (see below – although, given the powerful influence of Unite in Corbyn's Labour, Momentum's relationship with the Trade Union movement is not straightforward).

The political implications of that model for internal democracy are obvious. It is based on the line that the vanguardists have the key to history and understand the needs and demands of what they call the rank and file[48] better than they do themselves. It follows from this that the cohorts of new members are not there to provide any political initiatives; they are there, in their thousands, essentially to legitimise the activities of the vanguardists. The party membership are there to endorse, not challenge, the views of the vanguard; the Leninist model is wholly incompatible with the idea of a "member-led" party. Moreover, the model requires that the electorate are to be led and patronised, not engaged with; the relationship to the electorate becomes a matter of tactics, not one of political principle. And, finally, the vanguard party can rationalise its behaviour in the light of the alleged false consciousness of its opponents; and not just their false consciousness, because it is apparently necessary to demonstrate that they are not just wrong, but acting in bad faith. It is an explanation of the vituperative language in which such political discourse is often conducted.

<u>Democratic centralism and the establishment of Momentum</u>

Since the election of Jeremy Corbyn as Labour leader – and in particular through the establishment of Momentum as a group within the party, drawing on the mailing list of Corbyn supporters gathered during the leadership election campaign. Momentum's description of itself is:

---

[48] The term "rank and file" is military in origin and refers to the formations adopted by soldiers – not officers – on the parade ground. Its implications are obvious; the members of the "rank and file" are obviously subordinate, take no individual initiative, and act as one in obedience to orders. In a Labour movement in which the growth of identity politics has led to the careful use of language, the persistence of this term is revealing.

[49] https://peoplesmomentum.com/about/

Momentum is a people-powered, vibrant movement. We aim to transform the Labour Party, our communities and Britain in the interests of the many, not the few.

Our proposition is simple: if more of us come together, we can use our skills and energy to tackle every challenge head on. Using our collective power, our campaigning, networks and tech, we can transform society for the better.
From our view of the Labour Party, to how we change Britain for the better, we're up front about where we stand[49].

While Momentum talks about grass-roots democracy, and has a constitution that is in theory at least democratic, it is in fact a privately-owned company, with founder Jon Lansman as its sole shareholder; part of a web of businesses[50] owned by Lansman, an independently wealthy long-standing activist on the left, a former adviser to Tony Benn and Michael Meacher. It originated in the Corbyn campaign for the Party leadership, and aimed originally to continue the support for Corbyn within the Party in the belief that he would face a fundamentally hostile reception as he sought to put a more radical agenda into effect.

It is clear from their track record that Momentum sees itself – and is regarded by others – as Jeremy Corbyn's vanguard movement, and keeper of the Corbyn party's ideological soul. Its tactics have revolved around seeking control of Constituency and Branch Labour Parties – the fundamental grass-roots building blocks of the Labour Party's structures. It has in particular sought to control the selection of candidates for both Parliament and local government – with varying degrees of success.

It is important to understand that, however close some of its organizational methods may be to entryist forebears like Militant, Momentum is not an entryist group. There is nothing secret or closet about its operations; Momentum groups are active and visible, often using social media to further their campaigns[51]. It openly proclaims that it has recruited around more than 40,000[52] members – or about one

---

[50] A useful summary of Momentum's history can be found at https://www.buzzfeed.com/jamesball/inside-the-complex-snarl-of-companies-which-control-the-pro?utm_term=.mmRrkKwdLB#.tcROvpD52r

[51] https://www.theguardian.com/politics/2018/mar/18/revealed-how-increasingly-powerful-momentum-is-transforming-labour

in ten of the new members that have joined Labour since the Corbyn election campaign.

While Momentum has become the dominant force on the Corbynist left – in terms both of numbers and influence, it is certainly not the only group that wields influence. As we have seen, many of those around Corbyn are drawn from the Labour Representation Committee (LRC), a group associated particularly with John McDonnell, who remains its President.

Relations between Momentum and LRC have at times been difficult. In particular, the LRC criticised Momentum over a series of rule changes that it deemed to undermine the democratic structures of the organization, in particular the requirement that members and officers of Momentum should be full Labour Party members[53].

One of the more intriguing conflicts within the Left has been about the role of the trade unions. The Unite union and its General Secretary, Len McCluskey, have been prominent in their support for both Momentum and Corbyn's leadership. But that relationship has not always been easy. At one point Jon Lansman appears to have been talking about the possibility of forging formal links with Unite[54]. But other Momentum figures, including former Labour NEC member Christine Shawcroft, have been openly critical of the long-standing link between Labour and the Unions[55] – seen by many as being absolutely fundamental to Labour's structure and history, but which sits uneasily with the purer, more Leninist strands of organisation advocated by some in the Labour Party. More recently, relations between Lansman and Unite

---

[52] http://www.heraldscotland.com/politics/16137773.Momentum_membership_has_topped_40_000_members___making_it_bigger_than_Greens/

[53] https://labourlist.org/2017/01/labour-represenation-committee-takes-aim-at-momentum-over-controversial-member-reforms/

[54] https://www.theguardian.com/politics/2017/mar/18/secret-tape-reveals-momentum-plot-to-link-with-unite-seize-control-of-labour

[55] https://www.theguardian.com/politics/2018/mar/07/momentum-backed-nec-member-christine-shawcroft-labour-should-cut-union-links

[56] https://www.theguardian.com/politics/2018/feb/28/momentum-bid-for-key-labour-post-exposes-tension-with-unite

[57] https://labourlist.org/2018/08/were-campaigning-for-momentum-to-be-more-democratic-heres-why/

became strained when Lansman sought to be appointed as General Secretary of the Labour Party[56].

More recently, activists within Momentum have started to campaign for rule changes to open up its structures to greater control and influence from the membership[57]. The issue resurfaced in August 2018 when the Momentum leadership took the decision to drop Pete Willsman – a prominent figure in both the LRC and the Campaign for Labour Party Democracy – from its slate for the Labour NEC elections[58], over comments he made about antisemitism at an NEC meeting, among other things alleging that "Trump fanatics" in the Jewish community were concocting allegations about antisemitism to undermine Corbyn; comments that were recorded and later published in the Jewish Chronicle[59]. While many of the Momentum big names – people like political commentator Owen Jones and former Corbyn spokesman Matt Zarb-Cousins[60] – supported the decision, others strongly opposed it. Momentum groups around the UK, including the national Momentum affiliate in Wales, Welsh Labour Grassroots, urged members to continue backing Willsman – although they appear to have been reluctant to publicise the fact[61].

However, there is some evidence that Momentum is itself confused about its role, and, as part of a movement that is itself diverse, has been involved in activities that do not sit comfortably with its vanguard role.

One of the more extraordinary initiatives was the launch, in 2016, of a group called Momentum Kids, an organisation that had two purposes: to provide childcare for Momentum members, to allow those with children to participate more fully in political activity; and to provide an environment in which children could be engaged in politics[62].

---

[58]   https://www.newstatesman.com/politics/staggers/2018/08/momentum-dump-peter-willsman-their-nec-slate-direct-defiance-jeremy-corbyn

[59] https://www.thejc.com/news/uk-news/bombshell-recording-proves-corbyn-ally-blamed-jewish-trump-fantatics-for-false-antisemitism-clai-1.467802

[60] https://labourlist.org/2018/07/corbynites-urged-to-drop-support-for-peter-willsman-over-antisemitism-comments/

[61] Welsh Labour Grassroots reasserted their support for Willsman in an email message sent to members, but did not set out this position on their website or Twitter feed – see https://www.theredroar.com/2018/08/momentum-splinters-as-lansman-backlash-deepens/

[62]   https://labourlist.org/2016/09/momentum-kids-aims-to-make-politics-child-friendly/

Its launch provided much criticism and no little ridicule – images of solemn young children in red scarves being led on earnest nature rambles, or posing with Uncle Joe, were never far from the public consciousness. Indeed, some of the publicity around the launch, at the 2016 World Turned Transformed festival, did little to stem the ridicule: a linked event called "The Teddy Bear Mandate[63]", in which children were invited to bring a favourite toy and imagine which party it might belong to, and to ask questions about its mandate and how it would use that mandate to effect positive change, and to involve the toy in a mock protest complete with banners and songs, did little to dispel the sense of preciousness (as well as raising the obvious question – what if Teddy was a Blairite? Or even a Liberal Democrat?)

And the childcare issues, obviously, are problematic. Obviously, childcare is an important issue in broadening participation in politics, and initiatives that lower barriers to participation matter. However, childcare raises regulatory issues. There are questions of child ratios, and the fact that any provider offering more than two hours' childcare must be registered and open to inspection. Those providing childcare need to be subject to DBS checks. While it's easy to caricature the idea of bourgeois lackey social service departments sending in social workers to break up the vanguard of the revolution[64], there are obviously safeguarding issues that this kind of well-meaning amateurism may struggle to address.

Well-meaning amateurism also characterises another Momentum initiative – that of providing support for people who are facing difficulties with the Department of Work and Pensions over benefit claims – and in particular who may be challenging a reduction in their benefits as a result of a work capability assessment, or who may be sanctioned.

The point is that fighting a DWP decision successfully is not easy. A Benefit Tribunal is a Court hearing, managed by the Courts and Tribunal Service, and requires a similar degree of preparation and level of evidence. There is no doubt that there is a desperate lack of support for those people who are challenging DWP decisions and fighting for their legal right to the correct level of benefits; especially as the voluntary sector appears to have largely withdrawn from advocacy (in

---

[63] https://twitter.com/Momentum_kids/status/777814778760859648

[64] And it is worth noting that there is an ideological strand in some parts of the Left that social workers enact a class agenda, acting to disempower working-class communities.

particular for those with mental health issues), and that the Citizens' Advice Bureaux
– overworked, underfunded and lacking in expertise – are wholly unable to deal
with the volume of work the Work Capability Assessment system generates.
Government figures show that around 68% of cases that go to Tribunal are won by
the appellant[65] – but equally, it is clear that no more than a tiny proportion of cases
go all the way to tribunals, given the huge organisation obstacles that are placed in
their way. The need for proper support in the face of what is widely perceived to be a
brutal and failing system is obvious.

However, equally, it should be absolutely clear that it is wholly wrong for
amateurs, possibly off the back of a couple of hours of training from a CAB
volunteer, to try and give people hope that they can solve their problems. To the
extent that these volunteers are acting as recruiters for Momentum, their actions
are, quite simply, cynical and exploitative.

Far from being the activities of a vanguard acting as the ideological heart of a
political movement, these initiatives seem closer to David Cameron's idea of the "Big
Society" than to any Socialist conception of effecting social change; we are firmly in
the world of middle-class do-gooding that Orwell ridicules in *The Road to Wigan Pier*.
They fuel the sense that we are dealing not with political radicalism as such, but
what is actually a quite conservative form of feel-good benevolence which is more
concerned with personal validation than bringing about political change. It is
ultimately self-regarding rather than other-regarding.

Obviously, these kinds of initiatives appear to conflict strongly with the Leninist
model that Momentum and the Corbyn party appear to adopt in other ways. It
tempts one to argue that what is in play here is not so much Leninism, but Leninism
with muddled tendencies; that the tension between the democratic centralists and
the localists remains unresolved.

However, the nature of the conflicts will become clearer when we consider the
politics of the wider Corbynist movement. It is to them that we now turn.

---

65   https://www.mirror.co.uk/news/politics/victories-people-appealing-
disability-benefit-12149291

WHO ARE THE CORBYNISTS? AND WHAT DO THEY BELIEVE?

The purpose of this chapter is to answer two questions.

First, who are the Corbynists? Who are the people who flocked to the Corbyn banner in 2015, and who have apparently been politically energized by the new movement?

Second, what are their belief systems? What are the values and ideological assumptions that they bring to the Party, especially those who have not been involved in Labour politics before?

In short, while the previous chapter considered the ideology of the experienced politicians on the Left – and the role of the 30,000 Momentum members - this chapter will examine the wider ideals and practices of the new mass membership; what I shall refer to as the "Corbyn cohort".

<u>Who are the new members?</u>

Research by Poletti, Bale and Webb for the ESRC-supported Party Members Project into the new Labour members who joined after 2015 shows that, contrary to what is widely believed, they are neither significantly younger or working class than their pre-2015 comrades. According to a summary of the research published by the LSE[66] the average age is roughly the same, and incomes are slightly – though not significantly - lower. There are, however, significant differences: an increase in the proportion of women and a greater tendency to self-identify as left-wing.

Three differences stand out. The first is how members participate in politics. Old and new members were roughly equally likely to participate in online political activity, through Facebook and Twitter; but the new members are much less likely to undertake other, more traditional forms of political activity – apart from Momentum members, who, as well as being those who are most likely to undertake online activity, are also more likely than older members to have attended public meetings.

The second difference is that the new members believe much more strongly than older members that they are respected by the Party leadership. Indeed, three-quarters reported that they had joined explicitly to support the leadership – a far higher proportion than the pre-2015 members.

The third – and potentially most interesting - difference is that the new members are substantially more likely to be members of the "educated left-behinds" - people whose earnings are less than their level of education would lead one to predict. Relative Deprivation Theory predicts that people are prone to evaluate their economic success or failure by measuring against those with similar levels of educational achievement; the level of university graduates earning less than the average salary is ten percentage points higher (51% against 41%) among newer than older members, leading Poletti, Bale and Webb to speculate that Corbyn's appeal extends particularly to those who feel that they have not achieved their legitimate professional expectations.

One can draw a number of conclusions from this.

First, the usual line that the Corbyn surge has brought a new generation into politics, and energised people who have not hitherto been involved in politics, doesn't withstand scrutiny. Demographically, the Corbyn cohort is identical to the pre-2015 Labour party; this is no movement of the underprivileged or dispossessed. The demographics do not suggest a particularly radical party. What is different is the way in which they self-identify – how membership is about how they perceive themselves, and about personal loyalty to a leader.

---

66 http://blogs.lse.ac.uk/politicsandpolicy/explaining-the-pro-corbyn-surge-in-labours-membership/

Second, there appears to be an honest and sincere belief among new members that they matter – that the leadership is on their side, and will listen to them. They believe – to a greater extent than pre-2015 members – that they have influence. The rhetoric of a member-led party has clearly had an impact.

Third – and related to this - is the evidence that the Corbyn cohort are people who may have a sense of personal grievance; that, although their demographic remains largely similar to pre-Corbyn membership, and they are, by the standards of the population as a whole, well-educated and reasonably well-off, they have a sense that the world has not been kind to them.

A rather different take is given by an Election Data poll commissioned from YouGov[67] and published in March 2017 (i.e. six months after Corbyn was re-elected Labour leader, with fieldwork done in the middle of the preceding month). This suggests that in political, rather than demographic, terms, there are significant differences between the old and new Labour members. This poll shows that of pre-2015 members, only 28% approved of Corbyn's leadership, while the approval rating among new members was 69%. Most interestingly, Corbyn's approval rate was only 47% among Party members who voted Labour in 2015, but 73% of those who voted for other parties at the time. That compares with an almost even split between those who thought Corbyn was doing well (51%) and badly (47%). The message is that, regardless of demographics, there was a clear divide between those who had come into the Labour Party – especially those who had cast their votes elsewhere before joining the Party after 2015.

<u>What is the political practice of Corbyn cohort?</u>

One of the most interesting critiques of Corbynism is that set out by David Hirsch in a paper entitled *The Corbyn Left: the politics of position and the politics of reason.*[68] His central thesis is that contemporary left politics is more concerned with "othering" its opponents than winning them over. Opponents are regarded as being outside what Hirsch describes as "the community of the good" and therefore are not amenable to argument or reason; their failure is essentially a personal one. Obviously, in a Parliamentary democracy in which elections are won parties increasing their vote from outside their committed base, that has profound consequences for political method.

---

[67] http://election-data.co.uk/labour-membership-poll-results-2017

[68] http://fathomjournal.org/the-corbyn-left-the-politics-of-position-and-the-politics-of-reason/

Equally, obviously, how that community of "good" is defined is crucially important. And it follows that the community need not be a progressive one; such a narrative can be an intensely conservative one. The common ancestry with the more extreme forms of blood-and-soil nationalism will be obvious, as well as how this approach lends itself to cultism; it provides a rationale that binds together a group that sees itself as enlightened in a hostile world.

As Hirsch points out, Hannah Arendt argued that one of the defining features of totalitarian politics was the portrayal of political disagreements as originating, not in rational argument, but in social or psychological factors beyond the control of reason; providing a rationale for condemning the person, not critiquing their thinking. It becomes a matter of knowing better what you are against, rather than what you are for; it risks focusing discourse on the common enemy rather than the commonality of what you believe within the community of the good.

Conversely, it allows a political criticism to be reinterpreted as a personal attack. It explains the paradox that Corbyn has always stressed his opposition to personal attacks as part of his politics, while his supporters – especially on social media – are quite prepared to use personal criticism and ad hominem tactics such as "pile-ons" – a form of mobbing in which Corbyn supporters are encouraged by prominent pro-Corbyn social media commentators to attack critics. And one effect of this approach is that gives a rationale for *avoiding* political debate, a reason for declining to engage with critics.

Moreover, such an approach can lead to simplistic politics, related more to the group dynamic than an empirical understanding of the world around them. The lack of rootedness is shown in the Corbynistas' approach to political discourse. It is a discourse that often suggests they are more comfortable dealing with concepts than issues; happier making sweeping statements about "austerity" or "neoliberalism" than in discussing the realities of issues like falling pay, food banks or changes to benefits, except insofar as such things can be used to attack their opponents for being "neoliberal" – especially when one looks at the language of Corbyn's social media warriors.

In other words, they all too often fall prey to the fallacy of reification[69]: of investing what are generally abstract concepts with a concrete reality. As a party made up of a closed circle of largely privileged individuals with similar political

---

[69] https://en.wikipedia.org/wiki/Reification_(fallacy)

priorities, the abstractions are more "real" than the daily realities of those outside their immediate social ambit.   And it means that political discourse becomes related to buzzwords or simple slogans, which take the place of reasoned arguments. Vaclav Havel wrote about how, under Czech Communism, the simple act of displaying a placard in, say, a shop window stating "workers of the world unite", the shopkeeper was not just demonstrating loyalty to the Communist regime, but sending a whole series of messages about their own personal loyalties and "soundness"[70]

Hirsch argues that a key characteristic of this style of politics is that position is privileged over achievement; what defines a person's politics is whether they have taken the right positions to be included within the community of good. It is, in essence, more important that you use the correct forms of language than that you make serious attempts to bring about change; at one level the use of the correct language becomes the change.   At its least constructive that can become an obsession with identity politics or the politics of "not in my name" - which is all about me rather than about the situation. It can all too easily become a politics of feeling good about oneself and basking in the approval of being one of the elect. To use a term that is gaining increasing currency, politics becomes a matter of virtue signalling.   It becomes a way of absolving oneself of any complicity in the way the world is. But it's arguable that the whole point of taking part in politics is to get stuck into the process of effecting change, not complacently accepting that the state of affairs is someone else's problem. There is a fundamental paradox in play here, and it is one that the politics of Corbynism is replete with; that if you accept the "community of good" argument a personal attack on your enemy is not only justified but inevitable.

It also begs important question about the goodwill of your opponent. Because they are not of the "community of the good", they can become caricatured as conspiring to undermine the common good, because why else would people want to remain outside such a community? Effectively, they have decided to be "bad". Moreover, if you believe in a crude version of Marxism in which Socialism is inevitable, the product of social forces over which no individual has any power, then – quite obviously – the main criticisms against your opponents are either that they are ignorant, or that they are quite deliberately trying to interfere with the progress of history in a quite conscious - if necessarily futile – way.

---

[70] Havel, Vaclav *Living in Truth*

And when politics becomes that solipsistic, criticism becomes something other than a process of furthering understanding through debate and dialectic; it becomes a personal assault, and the reaction it provokes resembles that.

And it's arguable – as Lenin himself would have recognised – that such an approach to politics is fundamentally infantile; it is more interested in moralistic opposition than in effecting change[71]. It is infantile in a precise sense; like the small child who has yet to develop ego and superego and remains in thrall to the id, it is a politics that becomes a matter of visceral sensation, not reflection or understanding. And it is not surprising that it finds its most satisfying expression in the form of the mass political rally, the joining as one with a mass of similar-minded people and convincing oneself that it is that assembly, not the mass of Blairites, centrists, and falsely-conscious outside the hall who are reality. In a world of false consciousness, one can be part of the crowd of the enlightened and truth-seeking – and hence feel good about oneself, and even more fully alive.

Hirsch argues that for the Corbynist Labour Party, that "community of the good" expresses itself through a determination to be "anti-imperialist". Obviously, anti-imperialism has been a key strand of socialist practice, especially in Britain with its Empire past. But Hirsch describes anti-imperialism as operating in a very specific sense; one which has its roots in a concept of the United States as the world's principal imperial power, and which frames the good in terms of whether or not it is opposed or supportive of the material and military ambitions of the United State.

At the heart of that definition is the status of Israel, which is regarded as the United States' key ally and surrogate in the Middle East; and, alongside that, the status of the Palestinian people. The position that is taken on Israel, Palestine and the United States is at the heart of whether one is regarded as belonging to the community of the good. And this is one reason why antisemitism has become so closely associated with Corbynism – especially insofar as Israel is conflated with Zionism and the wider Jewish community. This aspect of Corbynism will be explored at length in Chapter 8 below.

---

[71] Lenin's book Left Wing Communism – An Infantile Disorder?, published in 1920, is mainly concerned with criticising those in the Socialist movement who refused to work with existing institutions including the Labour Party in Britain. Lenin argues that although the movement has already won over the "vanguard" of the working class, it needed to work with other political organisations in order to win over the masses.

The "community of good" argument is equally applicable to economic and social policy. The key word here is "neoliberal": the Left claims to be unequivocally opposed and "neoliberal" is one of the defining binary terms that it uses to define those – including many in the Labour Party – who are defiantly outside the immediate community of good. Neoliberalism is a term that is not often defined – its meaning is quite nuanced – but ii its content-free, reified form it is something that everyone inside the Corbynist community of good would want to be against; and it is of course easier for a community of good to define what it is against rather than what it is for. Insofar as one accepts any tenets of market economics, or even the idea of a mixed economy, or even that one has uttered words of criticism of John McDonnell - one is on the side of the neoliberals.

And Corbyn himself epitomises the politics of position. During more than thirty years in Parliament before becoming leader, Corbyn achieved nothing in the usual political sense. He never held any kind of office, never even proposed a Private Members' Bill, and was notable most of all for his record of having voted more than 400 times against his own Labour Government. According to a number of sources, his Parliamentary attendance was poor; for example no more than occasionally attending the regular Monday meetings of the Parliamentary Labour Party. While he was long recognised as a diligent constituency MP, he was not engaged with Parliament – and the politics of achieving change through Parliamentary politics[72].

But this lack of serious political engagement – combined with his readiness to appear on platforms for all sorts of "correct" causes – defines him, not as disengaged, but as a man of principle who has always been on the right side of history.   In the world of politics of position, the failure to engage with the sometimes messy and difficult world of practical politics, the world of trade-offs and compromise and real world constraints, is seen not as an evasion but as a model of behaviour.

It will be clear from the above that the politics of position, and of the "community of good", is not necessarily – or even usually – associated with the politics of the Left. One can see the same dynamic at work in the politics of the alt-Right; in the politics of nationalism as exemplified by the Trump Presidency in the US, as well as in the discourse around Brexit in the UK, where the reified concept of "taking back control" has acquired a range of meaning and symbolism that goes well

---

[72] The principal published source for this account is Rosa Prince's book *Comrade Corbyn* (see bibliography) but is supported by private conversations with former Labour MPs, which confirm the accuracy of Prince's account.

beyond the words of this simple phrase. In other words, rather than acting as a critique of what might be regarded as the politics of late capitalism, or indeed of the politics of anti-intellectualism, it appears to derive from essentially similar intellectual roots.

<u>Corbynism and postmodernist discourse</u>

To examine the common roots between right and left, it is necessary to examine some of the key questions of contemporary philosophical discourse

Keynes famously wrote that even the most apparently practical of people are often unknowingly slaves to some defunct economist. Much the same is true of philosophy; even the least philosophical of people have their assumptions and views of the world shaped in some degree by the philosophical climate around them. So it is useful to consider the philosophical milieu that is likely to have shaped the perceptions of those on the Corbynist left; what they encounter at university, in their reading and conversation.

A useful way into the mindset of the Corbynist Labour Party is to understand how wider intellectual trends have pushed political discourse away from universal progressive values into a competition between competing narratives, in an intellectual world in which there is no longer any faith in universal values. The problem of universality is one that goes back as far as Plato – but the key philosophical figures are Hume and Kant, who struggled with the fundamental problem that it is not, in principle, possible to be certain about anything. Descartes argued in his famous formulation "cogito ergo sum" that one could be certain of the existence of a thinking I, which gave a sense of certainty, but Locke and Berkeley challenged that belief. Induction - I.e. observation of repeated patters in nature - as Hume argues, gives us a useful guide to life but never one that creates real certainty; we never know when the counter-model arrives. Kant sought to define those things that could not be derived from observation – concepts like time, spatiality and so on – as "a priori" which derived from our mental structures, but they still locate reality firmly in the mind of the observer, not the object or phenomenon that is being observed.

In the twentieth century the debate about truth and reality shifted towards language – as expressed in the structuralism advocated by Althusser and the theories of discourse advanced by figures like Foucault and Barthes

But philosophical and political doubt are not the same thing – because politics is an activity that is, and indeed has to be, undertaken in a public world in which there need to be shared assumptions and values. Without shared assumptions and values, there is literally no such thing as society. Even if we accept that, as a matter of intellectual positioning, there is no such thing as truth or certainty, in a practical sense, in order to make any form of human society work, we have to rely on convention and practise as a way of making sense of, and acting in, that public world.

Moreover, the growth of postmodern thinking and the undermining of the grand narratives that follows from it has traditionally been seen as a liberating development, something that has instinctively appealed to the Left. It appears to challenge authority and allow for greater intellectual freedom and diversity. But in principle there is absolutely no reason why that should be the case, and increasingly it is understood differently, including on the Left; it is seen, first, as an ideology that fits closely with consumerism, in which individuals can pick and mix their narratives.

But it reflects one of the most important aspects of Marxist thinking – that *all* truth is ideological. The key passage occurs in *The German Ideology*, in which Marx argues[73] that the intellectual life of a society *must* derive from the organization of production, i.e. from its economic and class basis. Not, crucially, that it *may* do so, or that the economic and class system is one of the things that influences a society's culture – a proposition that few would dispute – but that it must do so. And, as Popper argues in *The Open Society and its Enemies*, that variety of thinking leads to a fundamental totalitarianism.

Similar problems arise with the practise of cultural studies, which has traditionally been associated with the Left (but events are showing that it can produce profoundly conservative narratives, which can have a seriously corrosive effect on the case for progressive political causes). Cultural studies involve a multidisciplinary and politically engaged examination of how meaning is bound up with, and generated by, cultural phenomena including systems of governance, control and oppression. Early cultural studies were based on the structuralism of thinkers like Althusser, and crucially on Gramsci's concept of hegemony.

---

[73] https://www.marxists.org/archive/marx/works/1845/german-ideology/index.htm

A crucial figure in this milieu is Foucault, who developed the work on semiotics of Saussure and Barthes, expanding the scope of meaning from symbols and signifiers to wider considerations of narratives, statements and groups of images – in other words, to discourses which allowed an understanding of social knowledge, social practices and, in particular, power. Foucault was concerned principally with relations of power, rather than meaning. Drawing on the Marxist heritage, Foucault was also concerned to historicise discourse – meaning arose only within a specific historical context. He emphasized that knowledge therefore must be enmeshed in relations of power; and, crucially, knowledge when linked to power not only gained authority but had the power to make itself true in a sense that produced a consensus that enabled social control – in other words, a *regime* of truth.

In other words – according to Foucault, and indeed to the wider movement of which he is part - the idea of truth is a social construct, and not objective at all. Truth becomes determined by social factors, by the narratives around one – a factor which led on to the adoption of cultural studies and identity politics; reality as a subjective phenomenon based on one's milieu.

The cultural studies movement has been criticised from both left and right – orthodox Marxists would argue that it places too much influence on cultural rather than economic factors at work in society, while those on the right believe that the influence of Marx on the development of cultural studies mean that its approach is fundamentally ideological.

Obviously, the grassroots Labour member who has joined the Party to support Corbyn, or the Momentum activist, is unlikely to link their political position explicitly to a relativist or postmodern form of discourse – even at a relatively crude level. But the point here is not to offer a critique of postmodernism, structuralism or cultural studies *per se* but to understand how they form the intellectual milieu in which a political movement of predominantly reasonably-well educated (I.e. sufficiently educated to have encountered these intellectual movements in the context, say, or an arts degree but perhaps not to have reached the level where they are concerned with critically analysing them[74]) and affluent supporters exists; in

---

[74] My own experience – having quite recently spent two terms doing an MA course as a mature student in an arts-related subject before deciding that it was not for me – is that, at least in the institution where I was studying, twentieth-century structuralism and postmodern theory are taught as the standard philosophical underpinning of the subject, with criticism of their influence neither invited nor tolerated.

other words, to understand the underlying intellectual assumptions that inform such people's approach to their politics, especially where the commitment is relatively casual, and even when those assumptions are based on crude or partly-digested versions of those intellectual positions.

It implies that their politics will be relativist in tone and will be based on an assumption that ideology is unavoidable; that any concept of truth involves an ideological position, and a historical one as well.   Most of all, it will incline their politics towards an essentially post-truth position.

Quite obviously, the Left has no monopoly on this approach; and that it informs much of what is described as "neoliberal" thinking, and in particular the alt-Right. One of the most outspoken critics of the postmodern and structural approach to politics has been Noam Chomsky, who has consistently argued that it has in fact provided a narrative of power, and has been used by the powerful to reinforce their power[75].

There is a notorious quotation that first appeared in the New York Times in 2004, attributed to a "senior White House adviser" in the George W Bush administration, and widely attributed to Karl Rove, which indicates how such a set of ideas can take root on the Right.   The comment was made by the staffer to the journalist who wrote the piece, which is about the way in which the Bush administration was essentially a "faith-based" rather than a "reality-based presidency:

> People like you are still living in what we call the reality-based community. You believe that solutions emerge from your judicious study of discernible reality. That's not the way the world really works anymore. We're an empire now, and when we act, we create our own reality. And while you are studying that reality—judiciously, as you will—we'll act again, creating other new realities, which you can study too, and that's how things will sort out. We're history's actors, and you, all of you, will be left to just study what we do[76].

The crucial phrase: "we create our own reality". In other words, politics is about faith and action, not empirical understanding. It's a style of discourse that will be

---

[75] https://www.newsclick.in/noam-chomsky-postmodernism-instrument-power
[76]   https://www.nytimes.com/2004/10/17/magazine/faith-certainty-and-the-presidency-of-george-w-bush.html

familiar to anyone who has dipped a toe into the murky philosophical waters of the works of Ayn Rand, whose influence on the American right has been enormous[77].

In discussing Karl Rove and Ayn Rand we are, superficially, in a different universe to the world of Corbynism – after all, this position comes from the heart of the administration that invaded Iraq, with Tony Blair as unflinching ally; the very antithesis of Corbynism, one might be tempted to think. But, as we have seen, the roots of the political method set out by the unnamed adviser are closer to the world of Corbynism than advocates of either would care to admit. The philosophical underpinning – that reality is something created rather than objective, something based on human agency in the face of social, political and historical circumstances – is fundamentally the same, even if Corbyn's supporters (for whom, of course, the idea of faith is by and large something very different to that obtaining on the Christian Right in the US) would emphatically reject that view.

But the fact remains that if politics is a collective activity, based on mutually-understood discourse, you have to have common standards of truth and veracity. Obviously that does not mean that one should not respect and seek to understand different cultural traditions and sets of values – indeed, a meaningful model of democracy that avoids the pitfalls of nationalism requires that you do so - but unless you are committed to wholly sectarian politics, you have to have some measure of objectivity. Democracy requires it; the alternative is a sort of racial or cultural nationalism, and it is obvious to anyone who understands the history of Europe in the nineteenth and twentieth centuries where that leads.

And the essential point here is that, like so much of the method of the alt-Right, Corbynism lies quite explicitly outside the liberal, objective and empirical political method, and which defines truth and reality in quite explicitly ideological terms. This is not to say that the liberal political discourse has not been coloured by ideology; quite the reverse. But the empirical method seeks consciously to identify and isolate the ideology, to understand that it is something that essentially corrupts and skews the discourse. But the postmodern political method, whether of left or right, despite its claim to reject the grand narratives, explicitly endorses and indeed

---

[77] For anyone wishing to gain some understanding of the strange work of Ayn Rand – part fiction, part cod philosophy, part outrageous egotism, and regarded by most serious philosophers as pseudo-philosophy but still hugely influential on the alt-Right, a review published in The Nation by Corey Robin gives a helpful (if far from impartial) introduction https://www.thenation.com/article/garbage-and-gravitas/

welcomes the skew; there is no discourse that is not ideological, and there is no point in trying to get away from it.

Obviously, Corbynism – and the postmodernism of the left generally - is different in the way in which it expresses itself that the postmodernism of the Right. It is more self-aware, more conscious of its educational heritage. It is more likely to find expression in the ranks of the academic community, because it reflects the assumptions of the privileged people within that community (as distinct from, say, the politics of the Tea Party Right in the United States, which regards that community as part of the problem of a politics that has left them behind).   The Left is probably better equipped, too, to use empirical narratives where that supports their values, e.g. on the issue of climate change.

<u>Corbyn and the media</u>

If there is one thing that appears to unite the Corbynist left (and the alt-Right too) it is a deep contempt for the mainstream media, which is frequently attacked for misrepresenting the Labour message – or for not covering events which they regard as significant. The usual narrative is that the media are biased, and represent an elite and "neoliberal" view of the world. There is of course an extensive literature that has explored the area of how both commercial and state media control the media (of which the writings of Noam Chomsky are perhaps the most widely cited).

Before discussing the criticisms from the Corbyn Left, it's worth saying that in most respects the media are the authors of their own misfortune. Most of the newspapers in the UK take a tendentious political line; many of them follow the populist Right, but even those that don't - like the Guardian - take a verbal bashing from the Corbynists on the ground of "centrism". The broadcast media, and especially the BBC, which is obviously far more heavily regulated than the print media, are also attacked. Once again, this criticism is far from coming solely from the left; traditionally the BBC has been lambasted from the Right for following what is believed to have been a liberal-left agenda, and it is currently under attack from those opposing Britain's departure from the EU on the grounds of being the "Brexit Broadcasting Corporation", acting as if Brexit were a done deal.

There is little doubt that the BBC must bear part of the blame. Standards of news broadcasting appear to have fallen. Listeners are deserting the Today programme on Radio 4 – once regarded as setting the day's news agenda – in their hundreds of thousands, and overbearing and tendentious interviewing from star journalists substituting their own opinions for objective reporting is widely being blamed[78].

More seriously, there has been growing criticism of what the BBC regards as "balance", where it is argued it has been willing to give equivalence between the overwhelming majority of the scientific community who back climate change and the small, politically- rather scientifically-motivated minority who believe it to be a hoax; or, for example, between a Professor of Medicine and a homeopath.

Their response has been to support independent left-wing websites like The Canary or the Skwawkbox, arguing that they are more reliable insofar as they carry reportage about the things that they would claim the BBC ignores. It's interesting that The Canary,[79] for example, displays prominently on its front page that it is registered with Impress, the independent news regulator; but there have been concerns about the essentially pay-per-click model it uses to pay its contributors.

But it is difficult to see how websites that – however openly – claim to support a particular point of view can, except in the ideological world described above, claim to be an antidote to a biased mainstream media.

More recently, following the announcement at the Edinburgh Television Festival of a range of policy proposals concerning the media[80], Corbyn has, using social media[81], offered a series of thoughts on "fake news" that appear to be close to those of Donald Trump – whose rhetoric uses that phrase repeatedly. His argument is that newspapers must be "democratized" – talking about "breaking the stranglehold of elite power and billionaire domination over large parts of our media", and claiming that "most people think that our newspapers churn out fake news, day in day out".

While it is difficult to see how a privately-controlled print media could be forced to allow journalists to elect editors without effectively ceding management of editorial control to state regulation, it appears that Corbyn's response is as much about replacing one essentially faith-based system with another, rather than tackling the root cause; and appears to be based on an assumption that political ideas are shaped by the media rather than the other way around, diminishing real experience. And – a point that will be explored more fully in Chapter 6 – this

---

[78]   https://www.theguardian.com/media/2018/aug/02/bbcs-today-programme-sheds-800000-listeners

[79] https://www.thecanary.co/values/

[80]   https://labour.org.uk/press/full-text-jeremy-corbyns-2018-alternative-mactaggart-lecture/

[81] https://twitter.com/jeremycorbyn/status/1032733580814950402

position seems to assume that what matters is a change of ownership, rather than engaging with the complexities and trade-offs around mass media in a digital age.

<u>Social media</u>

There is little doubt that Corbynism is a movement that has flourished partly as a result of social media, and which sees the use of social media as a key political technique. It's hardly surprising; a party whose intellectual roots lie in reified sloganizing and in the moral simplicities of being part of a community of good is particularly suited to the use of social media.

This is not the place for a detailed debate about social media. But, put very broadly, there are two conflicting views about its use[82]. The optimistic view is that it allows the empowerment of individuals, who are able to find freedom of expression outside social hierarchies. The pessimistic view is that, by encouraging unlimited consequence-free comment in forms that do not admit nuance or detail, it is encouraging a mob mentality; in an age when liberal norms are in decline, it accelerates and compounds that decline. Propositions are not discussed, or weighed evidentially: they are liked.

Both arguments have their merits. But blaming a medium for a wider social or political trend achieves nothing; and the problem with politics and social media is that in an environment in which norms of debate have been hollowed out by a wider flight from empiricism and nuance – and in which the nature of political discourse has become irrational and polarised – is that social media can act simply as an amplifier. The politics of irrationalism is a cause, not an effect, of the way in which social media are used; there is a reason why Donald Trump, who epitomises the authoritarian politics of irrationalism, is so indefatigable a user of Twitter.

And there is every reason why political movements rooted in distrust of the "mainstream media" should use forums like Twitter and Facebook; they would argue that they are able to get their message, unmediated, to the world that would otherwise be dependent on the distortions of the mainstream media; they can argue that the views expressed by Facebook and Twitter users are "authentic" in a way that those presented by the mainstream media are not. The problem, quite obviously, is that there is an enormous difference between assertion and argument.

[82] A short discussion of the different views can be found at https://theconversation.com/how-the-wisdom-of-the-crowd-can-turn-into-social-media-mob-rule-43376

And, equally obviously, assertion is much easier than argument in a medium where one is limited to 280 characters, or where one is simply looking to maximise the number of "likes", or for your hashtag or post to go "viral".

The use of hashtags and slogans illustrates a particular problem for the Corbynist left - the way in which its key slogans are devoid of meaning. Slogans have political traction – as one can see from how the phrase "taking back control" gained resonance beyond the immediate meaning of the words when, in the case of the 2016 EU referendum, they are used by canny (and many would say unscrupulous) politicians. But the phrases of Corbynism seem to be particularly meaningless. "For the many", for example, could just as easily have been used by Margaret Thatcher; its significance appears to lie less in its ability to attract new supporters but in the way it provides a shorthand by which the faithful can identify one another. Again, one could argue that social media provide the means to disseminate a really powerful form of words – although skilled media practitioners like Harold Wilson and Tony Blair showed they were more than capable of doing this before the invention of social media. However the experience to date of politics on social media will be taken by many as suggesting that Facebook and Twitter degrade rather than enrich political debate.

Corbyn and popular culture

One of the most-repeated claims about Corbyn's Labour is its ability to attract young people. As we have seen, claims that the surge in Labour's membership since 2015 is down to attracting young people are exaggerated – but at the same time it is clear that Corbyn resonates with young voters more clearly than any other contemporary British politician (with the possible exception of Caroline Lucas).

The way in which Corbyn has motivated a younger demographic is significant. I've already mentioned the link to Dumbledore; but the fact that Generation Corbyn has been reared on narratives like Star Wars, the Lord of the Rings and Harry Potter – dominated by benign paternalistic figures, Obi Wan Kenobe, Gandalf and Dumbledore, who closely resemble the Jungian archetype of the Wise Old Man. All three are overwhelmingly forces for good, and above all of stability in a troubled and disintegrating world caught in a Manichean struggle, often against conspiracies to undermine the good[83]; all are called upon to make the ultimate sacrifice (although

---

[83] It is notable that the Yougov survey of Corbyn supporters in the 2015 leadership contest referenced in Chapter 3 suggested that they were twice as likely as the population at large to believe that the world was run by a secretive elite:

Gandalf returns transfigured).   They are both insiders and outsiders – people of power, but whose principle has put them outside the dominant power structures. The emotional appeal to people who sense the unfairness and injustice of modern society but do not understand – or possibly seek to avoid - understand its complexity and its impermeability to easy solutions.

The point here is that, to the extent that one accepts the Jungian idea of the development of the psyche, Corbyn's supporters – weaned on a particular form of the Wise Old Man myth – are projecting parts of themselves on to Corbyn. They attend rallies, not to take part in a political process, but an emotional and psychological one; and this intense identification with their leader comes from the emotions that they are projecting on to him. It also helps explain their intensely hostile reaction to criticism on social media. What it clearly is not is an example of serious political and intellectual engagement.

And there are some theorists who have attempted to make an explicit link between Corbynism and the counter-culture, in an attempt to link Corbyn to such things as the rise of new-age consciousness and what is described as the "solidarity of the festival" - a body of theory that has acquired the title "Acid Corbynism", a phenomenon described by Jeremy Gilbert in a piece in Red Pepper[84] and expanded on in a piece on his own blog[85].

Gilbert argues that techniques of self-transformation like yoga, meditiation or psychedelic drugs could theoretically have a radical potential if they were linked to a wider culture of questioning capitalism and organising against it. Quoting Foucault, he argues that while these "technologies of the self" are politically neutral, they can form part of a milieu in which both traditional hierarchies and individualism can be challenged; and such techniques as consciousness-raising were at their peak in the 1970s when, he argues, the politics of the new left were at their most powerful. He argues that the hierarchies and institutions of capitalism inhibit creative or dynamic thinking, and so have an emotional effect; and links the idea of consciousness-raising to Marx's concept of class consciousness, in which the shared status of workers is more important than their personal or cultural status. Hence events that produce a collective feeling of joy can provide strength or inspiration for political

---

https://yougov.co.uk/news/2015/08/27/you-may-say-im-dreamer-inside-mindset-jeremy-corby/

[84] https://www.redpepper.org.uk/what-is-acid-corbynism/

[85]   https://jeremygilbertwriting.files.wordpress.com/2017/09/psychedelic-socialism2.pdf

radicals. Gilbert links this to the creation of collectives and workers' control in industry. He writes of Corbynism as part of a largely self-organised movement, with social media acting as the new technology of the self.

There are a number of obvious points to be made here. Gilbert states that the view widely held on the left – he cites Slavoj Zizek and Adam Curtis, but the view is much wider than that – that the counterculture of the 1960s onwards is essentially not a radical phenomenon, but a forerunner of crass commercialism, but does not attempt to rebut it. Moreover, he appears to be unaware of the idea of the tyranny of structurelessness; the way in which such apparently non-hierarchical movements in reality replicate the social structures around them, especially when - as in the case of Corbyn's supporters – they are drawn so heavily from the ranks of the entitled and privileged.

And, in quoting Foucault's idea of the technologies of the self, he misses the key point that although participation in activities like consciousness-raising may be collective, it's always ultimately an individual activity – about the personal rather than the collective; something that in his own definition Foucault makes abundantly clear[86]. Politics as an activity is about making collective decisions in order to produce change; for those on the political left, it involves doing so in the face of deeply entrenched structures of power and privilege. Ultimately there has to be a method – an agreed and democratic one – of making decisions, and taking responsibility for those decisions: and vague generalisations about consciousness-raising do not look like a credible political method; rather a way of *avoiding* politics.

And this brings us back to a fundamental issue – that this type of theorising is, ultimately, wholly individual: it is, to use the common phrase, about feeling good about oneself. The consciousness-raising of the 1960s – and since – is an entirely self-regarding act: it's the reason why so many of the flower children of the 1960s ended up backing Reagan and Thatcher. Ultimately, the freedoms sought in the 1960s were personal, and the political – by its very nature – is collective.

Turning to the contemporary politics of Corbynism, it is undoubtedly true that one of the iconic moments of Corbynism was Corbyn's appearance at Glastonbury in 2017[87]. Corbyn received a rapturous reception from a crowd of a size, as the

---

[86] https://foucault.info/documents/foucault.technologiesOfSelf.en/

[87] https://www.theguardian.com/music/2017/jun/24/jeremy-corbyn-calls-for-unity-in-glastonbury-speech

Guardian reports, that is normally reserved for headline acts at the Festival. However, Glastonbury, whatever its youthful and radical roots, has become a festival for the affluent, middle-aged and middle-class – the price of tickets dictates that it cannot be otherwise – rather than the young. To use Marxist terminology, it is difficult to argue that Glastonbury has not become wholly commodified[88], part of a strongly-commercialised festival "season" to which a certain type of the privileged flock in much the same sense that the aristocratic and wealthy flock to Glyndebourne, Henley and Cowdray Park.

To summarise: the politics of Corbynism reflects a particular political method, which is in turn based on a set of philosophical assumptions. Those assumptions are the same as the underpinning of movements on the alt-Right; they represent a rejection of the values of liberal empirical democracy, and in turn lead to a political method that is about assertion and belonging rather than reason and achievement. To that extent they represent a rejection of politics itself; which is why they are so suited to the bearpit of social media. And if this is true, it means that the main divide in contemporary politics is not between left and right, but between those who accept the political method that has supported liberal democracy, including social democracy, and the politics that undermines and attacks liberal democracy. And that Corbynism is firmly in the latter camp.

---

[88] A ticket to Glastonbury in 2017 cost £238 https://www.glastonburyfestivals.co.uk/2017-ticket-sale-faq/

IS CORBYNISM A CULT?

At the 2017 Labour Party conference in Brighton, a delegate paraded an icon of Jeremy Corbyn. A crude portrait, decorated with fairy lights and tinsel, was carried around the conference hall to the cheers of the assembled delegates, and chants of "Jeremy! Jeremy!". According to the Daily Mirror[89], onlookers noted both its similarity to religious iconography and to the images of Lenin paraded by his supporters in Red Square.

And it did not stop there: the same report describes how some Labour officials wanted Corbyn – literally – to walk on water at the same conference, by addressing crowds on the beach from a floating platform; officials – perhaps remembering Neil Kinnock's infamous tumble[90] during a conference-time walk along Brighton beach – appeared to have thought better of it.

And this was not an isolated reaction. A year earlier, during the Labour leadership contest between Corbyn and Owen Smith, the author J K Rowling[91] had had to face a torrent of online abuse when she declared – in the face of social media comment likening Corbyn to Hogwarts headmaster Professor Dumbledore – that there was no resemblance at all, citing Corbyn's contract with Iranian state TV as evidence to the contrary.

If there is perhaps one event that captures the spirit of Corbynism, it is the Labour Live event held in North London on 16th June 2018. Dismissively dubbed "Jezfest", it was designed to be a public festival of live music, food, togetherness and political action. Headline acts included middle-ranking (in terms of popularity) but

---

[89] https://www.mirror.co.uk/news/politics/someone-brought-light-up-jeremy-11232867

[90] https://www.youtube.com/watch?v=jh8ktNsie0I

[91] https://www.telegraph.co.uk/films/2016/08/31/jk-rowling-jeremy-corbyn-is-not-dumbledore/

appropriately on-message musical performers, mixed in with speeches from John McDonnell, Owen Jones, and of course Corbyn himself. All at a bargain price of £35 per ticket.

It was an event that appears to have been doomed from the outset - whose organisers grossly overestimated the level of demand, with the result that ticket sales had to be boosted by price reductions and offers of free tickets through the Unite union (an offer that was, by all accounts, abused on an industrial scale, with tickets issued in the name of Tony Blair, Pol Pot, Leon Trotsky and Aunty Semite, among others[92]). In the event about 13,000 tickets were issued and attendance was estimated to be around 6000 – less than a third of the number forecast. Estimates of the losses borne by the Labour Party on the event vary from £100,000 to £1million.

Reports in the media – including a piece in the Guardian[93] by Martha Gill that by all accounts earned her an avalanche of hate-Tweets - pointed out that this was anything other than a political event; it was a collection of predominantly middle-class people who seem to be indulging in a form of self-congratulatory fantasy politics; the point being that it was wholly inward-looking. There is no sense that elections are won by winning over people whose initial inclination is not to agree with you; that it's about looking outside your small tent.

These are just a few examples to show how allegiance to Jeremy Corbyn has gone beyond the normal boundaries of political loyalty. In an age when it is generally assumed that people have become more sceptical about politicians and the political process, Corbyn attracts an extraordinary degree of personal adulation, to the point where Corbyn's Labour is often described by its critics as a cult.

In many respects it's a surprising development. Jeremy Corbyn is not charismatic, and, during his leadership election in 2015, demurred from the idea that leader-figures mattered. He argued that it was the ideas, and the force of the leader's supporter, not the leader himself, that mattered. And, given Corbyn's political background, it's even stranger – he was, after all, for many years among the group of politicians associated with Tony Benn, who consistently argued that the media trivialised politics by reducing it to a competition between personalities rather

---

[92]   https://metro.co.uk/2018/06/14/jokers-have-hours-of-fun-sending-labour-live-tickets-under-offensive-and-funny-names-7632046/

[93]   https://www.theguardian.com/commentisfree/2018/jun/18/jeremy-corbyn-tories-little-fear-jezfest-labour-live

than a debate about issues. Corbyn is not a fiery platform orator, who can rouse an audience with rhetorical passion; his delivery is wooden (he has a poor sense for the shape of a phrase, the end often falling away) and even pedantic.

Moreover, personality cults are not usually considered a feature of democratic politics, being more suited to the more extreme authoritarianism of both Left and Right. And yet Corbyn enjoys an almost fanatical base of support – especially through social media, where to criticise him is often to attract a torrent of abuse.

Personality cults are nothing new in politics – even if they are rarely associated with democratic politics; they have formed the basis of authoritarian regimes of both the left and right. The usually resolve around a close identification between a strong charismatic leader and their supporters, in which the personality of the leader becomes a substitute for the political process. In other words, cults are almost by definition the antithesis of democratic politics.

That definition is consistent with accepted views on what constitutes a cult outside the sphere of politics. A variety of definitions exist, but the common features are:

- A group united by allegiance to a charismatic leader or leadership, uniting around an ideology that offers a comprehensive view of the universe.
- The group will be held together by providing a sense of safety for its adherents from what is perceived as a hostile world
- At the same time the need for conformity will mean that strict discipline is enforced within a cult, often maintained by a pervasive sense of fear;
- Members will always act in the interests of the cult, never their own
- Cult members will tend to regard those outside the cult as engaged in conspiracies against them.

The people who are attracted to cults tend to be vulnerable, often going through life-changing experiences. Isolation from previous relationships is a classic

---

94 Some useful material on cults can be found at https://www.ibtimes.co.uk/cult-recruitment-why-do-people-join-them-what-techniques-are-used-lure-them-1557303 and (although it's an old piece) https://www.nytimes.com/1982/03/15/style/the-psychology-of-the-cult-experience.html

condition. They are often young, intelligent, and come from affluent or sheltered backgrounds[94].

The warning signs that groups working to prevent young people being sucked into cults – or to support them when they choose to leave – include, typically, absolute authoritarianism with not tolerance of questioning or debate; an obsession with conspiracies, the group leader is a conduit for absolute truth that is beyond challenge; and a belief that opponents are malignant and organized.

It is not difficult to discover evidence of every one of these among the faithful: ten minutes on Twitter will be more than enough. The language has been binary and exclusive; either you are one of us, or one of the enemy, and the most dangerous enemy is that large part of the leader that is sceptical about, or challenging of, the words of Jeremy Corbyn. The tone from prominent Labour figures like Owen Jones and Paul Mason has moderated lately, to suggest that Labour still needs to be a broad church once again, but the message from the activist Tweeters remains the same; back Corbyn, or get out.

And the pro-Corbyn messages are revealing, as they tend not to be political at all, but personal. Typical phrases include:

Corbyn is a man of unshakeable principle
Corbyn has been on the right side of history
Corbyn has fought all his life against racism
Corbyn has decency and humanity

Which may be very well, but these are not political statements. They could be made of any politician, right or left, whose view of the world the speaker happens to share. It seems to be that this is no more than brand identification, a consumerist need to trumpet one's own identity.

Very often, Corbyn is the subject of memes – images often including text that are designed to make a simple visual political point. Some of these include the references to Dumbledore or Gandalf that we have already noted. Others include poems:

Softly spoken
Crooked tie
Cheery twinkle
In his eye

Union badge
Worn with pride
To let us know
He's on our side

Right wing press
Who are they?
With this man
They hold no sway

He's on a mission
To make things fair
To give us hope
And ease despair.[95]

This is not a book of literary criticism, but it is hard to avoid the comparison with the more mawkish and sentimental types of Victorian hymns, or the tragic (in every sense) muse of William McGonagall[96]. Whatever the case, it certainly isn't politics.

But it isn't a one-off either – it is possible to buy an entire book of Corbyn-supporting poetry[97]. Now there is a serious point that there is, on the Left, a long tradition of poetry and song to accompany political activity; marching songs and commemorations. But they were not saccharine tributes to individuals, but calls to action; their focus was collective, not the individual.

To be fair it's far from just being Corbyn. During the 2015 General Election campaign, I was part of Labour's campaign in Brighton Pavilion, and saw something very similar: not only did Green supporters and campaigners insist that Labour had no "right" to stand against Caroline Lucas, but voters in well-heeled parts of the constituency justified their support for Caroline Lucas on grounds of personality – including the person who said that she wanted Lucas elected even if that let the Tories in "because I love her"; the person who was voting for her because "she's such a nice person", or, most of all "because she has done so much for Brighton", at the same time that her Party was forming perhaps the most unpopular administration in the history of Brighton and Hove City council. When the Guardian

---

[95] https://imgur.com/r/ukpolitics/tzdKVSs

[96] http://www.mcgonagall-online.org.uk/

[97] http://www.shoestring-press.com/2016/09/poems-for-jeremy-corbyn/

uncovered a student in Brighton who had a shrine to Lucas in her bedroom[98], I don't think any of us in the Labour campaign were in the least surprised. Neither am I remotely surprised that social media photos of meetings supporting the Momentum Left's recent coup in the Brighton and Hove Labour party appear to be full of people who were active Lucas supporters and even Green Party members.

In other words, one could easily draw the conclusion that the politics of Corbynism are part of a more general – and fundamentally anti-democratic and anti-political phenomenon

<u>Cult or hobbyism?</u>

There is, however, an alternative view that, far from being an indication of fanatical support for Corbyn, the cultism is in some senses a symptom of political disengagement.

A paper by Eitan Hersch of Yale University[99] considers the reasons why people become involved in politics, and the implication of what he sees as a growing element of hobbyism in political activity. Hersch considers the reasons why people become involved in political activity, and lists three – civic duty, self-interest and for self-gratification, i.e. as a hobby. Hersch focusses on the nature of political activity and the different levels of personal satisfaction associated with it, and argues that political hobbyism has potentially difficult consequences; in particular a risk that participants will develop an unrealistic sense of priorities, as disengagement and the priorities of personal satisfaction lead to a risk that participants will confuse high- and low-stake activities. By comparing political identification with support for sports teams, he argues that for the political hobbyist, partisan identification operates at an emotional level, and becomes a way of managing one's own image. He makes a comparison between the Kennedy/Goldwater Presidential election of 1964 and the Obama/Romney election of 2012, and argues that the evidence shows that although the ideological divide was

---

[98] https://www.theguardian.com/education/2015/apr/09/green-party-voice-of-youth. As one of the stalwart members of the Brighton Pavilion Labour Campaign commented on the accompanying photo of Caroline Lucas' student supporters: "I was at Sussex in '68 and they look a pretty tame lot to me".

[99]

http://www.eitanhersh.com/uploads/7/9/7/5/7975685/hersh_theory_of_hobbyism_v2.0.pdf

much starker in 1964, paradoxically the activists appeared to believe that the outcome mattered more in 2012.

There are obvious questions that arise from this. One is that, despite the comparison between 1964 and 2012, he has relatively little to say about ideological motivation; another is that he writes about the US political system, where partisan identification has traditionally been less ideological than in Britain. Hersh makes it clear that he is identifying a research agenda rather than advancing a fulfilled thesis. But nonetheless, there are some big questions here for an understanding of the politics of Corbynism.

Hersh is interested in the relationship between activity and gratification. One of the most frequent complaints by old Labour stalwarts about the new Corbynist members is their reluctance to get involved in the heavy lifting of political activity; the door-knocking, the leafletting, the meetings. Traditional political engagement has been time-consuming and hard work; not just the many meetings of varying degrees of interest, but the day-to-day grind of canvassing; the rain, the aggressive dogs, the hills, the letter-boxes with strong springs that nip at your fingers, the people who are not slow to show their displeasure at a person with a red rosette appearing uninvited on their doorstep. Of course not all, or even most, Labour Party members have been engaged at that level; many simply do what they can at election campaigns, or donate money, or turn up to the quiz nights.

But the point is that all of this involves a greater degree of commitment – emotional and practical – than the new politics of social media activism, or even of turning up to rallies. It involves far more than liking Facebook posts, or taking part in Twitterstorms, or even longing for the day when one achieves the Socialist Nirvana of being retweeted by Owen Jones. Experienced campaigners know that social media has a role in rallying the faithful, but really isn't political campaigning at all. It's preaching to the converted[100]. But it is something that can be done from the comfort of your own home, or on the bus on your smartphone; it is an activity that you can do when you feel like it.

---

[100] It is important to note that this is not the same sort of activity as that undertaken by the Leave campaign during the EU referendum, with its use of targeted Facebook advertising. That is a much more professional, paid and nuanced undertaking, requiring research, data management, and especially resources; it has nothing in common with the casual activity of the social media warrior.

So obviously there is a paradox. On the one hand, you have people who show cultist behavior; and there are undoubtedly individuals who do exhibit the intense emotional identification and the suspension of individual judgement that cultism implies; and the emotional investment, such as it is, is in Corbyn as individual rather than the politics. But on the other hand, some of that behaviour is arguably not a symptom of cultism, but of the very opposite – of *disengagement.*

As we saw in Chapter 3, one of the characteristics of social media activity is that it is, by and large, consequence free – at least in the immediate term (although there is a growing number of examples where past indiscretions on social media have damaged careers – political and otherwise). And to get involved you don't really need to care very much; tweeting or liking is essentially a quick, content-free piece of virtue signaling; of showing the world whose side you're on.

So the answer is that cultism and disengagement are by no means mutually exclusive. A cult normally demands the complete immersion of the personality into the aims of the cult and the identity of the leader. It seems clear that this happens insofar as the the Corbynist social media warrior is engaged in politics; but also that politics only occupies a part of that social media warrior's life. Outside the small world of social media, it's irrelevant; and one could argue that even activity such as attending a rally the social media is still in that closed world, not the open world of political debate; sitting in the hall, perhaps, surrounded by hundreds of others, but reliving that experience by tweeting, and retweeting others in that audience who are similarly hunched over their smartphones. The sense of belonging is mediated through that smartphone, not by physical proximity. In that scenario, cultism is not the antithesis of disengagement; the two are intimately connected.

And that disengagement is all of a piece with the vanguard model of Party organization described in Chapter 4 above – because if you have activists whose emotional commitment does not extend towards the cyber-world, and politics extends no further than the taking of positions on social media, you have a ready-made army who will accept what the vanguard tells them what to do. The crucial point about the vanguardists at the centre of the Corbyn movement is not that they want to empower the mass membership of the party, but to ensure that they remain disempowered; they can vote the line but not set the agenda.

So, to bring the threads together, what are the roots of this combination of cultism and disengagement?

One very obvious answer is that it represents a loss of faith in the conventional democratic process; a belief, however dressed up in democratic language, that political change is better effected by a charismatic individual than through the messy politics of managing institutions and structures. People believe that the latter has been tried and shown wanting: ultimately there is a belief that "they're all the same", not helped by high-profile scandals like those relating to Parliamentary expenses.

But the problem is that the real world is messy, and is managed through institutions and structures and processes; and that political decisions often involve trade-offs between competing priorities. The collapse of faith in democratic institutions around the world is well chronicled, but cultism around Corbyn – and, during the referendum campaign, Boris Johnson and Nigel Farage – is a sign of how far what one might call the liberal politics of social democracy have been devalued. It's all of a piece with the contempt for experts that was voiced during the EU referendum campaign; people yearn for simplicity and, in the case of Brexit, for a less confusing and less uncertain past. The great advantage – in terms of the emotional contentment of the individual – is that trusting in an individual is easier, more comforting than political discourse and decision-making. And ultimately history tells us that political cults in office (not that Corbyn appears to have much chance of achieving that) do not end well. Those who believe in rational politics have a lot of work to do.

But, also, it's possible to see the combination of cultism and disengagement as a politics of entitlement – a politics that is not about changing the world, or delivering in office, but about making the participant feel good about themselves. It's at heart a deeply consumerist – even (to the extent the term means anything) a neoliberal – approach to politics; cheerleading a brand rather than creating an open rational dialogue, and using the methods of puffery and advertising. And again, the contempt for expertise is part of this – it's a politics of self-indulgence, and none the less so for its rootedness in an often superficially well-educated and professional, well-heeled part of the population. The problem with consumerist politics, of course, is that you can't take a government back to the shop for a refund; something that people are beginning to learn the hard way after the EU vote. It's always someone else who picks up the political tab for populism gone bad.

Ultimately, this kind of politics – combined with the undoubted influence of a resurgent hard-left that is finding its way back into the Labour Party, small in numbers but organised and effective – is simply no challenge to entrenched structures and institutions. British politics, post-2007 crash and post-Brexit vote, is in a very fluid state and, to the extent that the polls are right, people are trusting the Tories to deal with the chaos that they have themselves wrought. And it's not party activists, or members, but sceptical people sitting on their sofas in marginal constituencies that we have to win over; and they're just not interested in helping well-heeled activists feel good about themselves, or about quasi-doctrinal disputes conducted by people hurling 280-character abuse on social media.

And, most of all, the combination of cultism and disengagement is deeply inimical to the ideal of rational, empirical politics. While social media hobbyism gives the appearance of political engagement, it is absolutely the opposite of political empowerment; and, as such, it is giving the existing structures of power and privilege a free pass.

CORBYN'S ECONOMIC POLICIES: FOR THE MANY?

As the earlier chapters made clear, one of the most important parts of the appeal of Corbyn's Labour lies in its challenge to the economic consensus of the Coalition years between 2010 and 2015, and its refusal to accept the coalition agenda. Corbynist rhetoric is largely about a more equal society, one that is fairer and in which extremes of wealth and privilege are at least mitigated, if not eliminated – a society that is "for the many".

Moreover, Labour had to tackle the abiding problem that the economy was its Achilles heel; it remained associated with "tax and spend" and clearly had much to do to retain electoral credibility. The Ed Balls strategy of working within a Conservative-defined fiscal framework had obviously failed; a perceived shift to the Left meant that the attacks would be all too predictable.

So how far does Corbyn's Labour really take this principle? In practice, how radical is its economic policy? How credible is it?

The 2017 Labour Manifesto made a series of commitments as to how Labour would run the economy. Its main elements were:

- Substantial increases in public investment;
- Increases in current public expenditure;
- Increases in taxation, including increased corporation taxation and an expansion of the top income tax band;
- The nationalisation of rail operators, water and electricity suppliers[101];

---

101 https://www.bbc.co.uk/news/election-2017-39933116

As a response from Paul Johnson of the Institute of Fiscal Studies argued, the issue with the manifesto commitments was not so much one of costing them, but understanding that they would lead to some fundamental changes in the operation of the UK economy[102]. He argues that the core pledge to increase borrowing to fund investment by £25bn was affordable, but it was difficult to assess whether the substantial costs of bringing utilities into public control would be. Current spending increases - £10bn for the abolition of tuition fees, £8bn for schools and further education, £6bn (which Johnson describes as "modest") for the NHS. Rises in corporation tax, in income tax for the top 5% of earners, and this would undoubtedly lead to a much larger state than had been seen for decades: add the effect of increases in minimum wages – which would effectively mean the Government was responsible for setting the pay of a quarter of private sector workers and half young workers, and that manifesto would mean a fundamental change to the economic role of the state. At that level, at least, the policy matches the rhetoric; Labour's proposals were both fundamental and achievable. And they reflected a decisive move away from the austerity mindset that constrained Labour before 2015.

However, in other ways the Labour manifesto remained relatively conservative. For example, it would only restore some £4bn of a total of £11bn of benefit cuts already in the pipeline[103]. And McDonnell had attracted some criticism from supporters by his adoption of a fiscal rule in which he argued that day-to-day public spending would be subject to "iron discipline"[104], with tax revenues and current spending balanced over the life of a Parliament, combined with a promise to reduce the overall level of Government debt (and therefore ensuring that in theory McDonnell's fiscal rule was actually tougher than Gordon Brown's as Chancellor). However, in practice a proviso that the rule would be abandoned when interest rates were at, or close to, zero.

Shadow Chancellor John McDonnell has made it very clear that stimulating investment is a crucial part of Labour's programme. And he is right to do so – the UK economy has been caught in a vicious circle of low investment and low

---

[102] https://www.ifs.org.uk/publications/9218

[103] A complete set of slides from the Institute of Fiscal Studies comparing the effect of Labour and Conservative 2017 manifesto commitments can be found at https://www.ifs.org.uk/uploads/Presentations/Carl%20Emmerson%2C%202017%20 General%20Election%2C%20manifesto%20analysis.pdf

[104] https://www.theguardian.com/politics/2016/mar/10/labour-seeks-to-win-back-partys-reputation-for-economic-competence

productivity. McDonnell's estimates of fiscal multipliers are rather conservative – rather more so than those used by the IMF[105].

McDonnell's adoption of the fiscal rule was probably overshadowed at the time by his decision to brandish Mao Zedong's Little Red Book in Parliament in response to George Osborne's spending statement[106]. But perhaps one could see this as an example of the old tactic of dressing up a conservative statement in radical clothing.

And, for all the radical positioning, McDonnell's proposals – save for the nationalisations – are relatively conservative; indeed, his fiscal rule has been attacked by Richard Murphy, a former member of McDonnell's panel of economic advisers as being far *too* conservative[107]. This is very much a return to an old-fashioned Keynsian approach to demand management, especially at a time when interest rates are so close to zero, allowing so little scope for monetary stimulus, and when years of neglect of public investment mean that the multiplier effect – the knock-on effect of public borrowing as it works through the economy – is likely to be relatively high.

The nationalisation proposals are more controversial. Public ownership, obviously, is at the heart of Labour's programme – railway operations, water, and energy would all be brought back into public ownership, with McDonnell claiming that it "would not cost the taxpayer a penny" - an extraordinary claim given that the Social Market Foundation, in a report commissioned by water companies, estimated that the up-front cost of nationalising the water industry alone would be around £90bn[108]. McDonnell argues that this would be taking an asset into ownership, which would then generate an income.

The key text is a speech that McDonnell gave to a Labour conference on alternative models of ownership in February 2018[109]. In that speech he set out both

---

105   https://www.channel4.com/news/factcheck/factcheck-john-mcdonnell-doesnt-seem-to-understand

106   https://www.theguardian.com/politics/2015/nov/25/john-mcdonnell-mao-zedong-little-red-book-george-osborne

107   http://www.taxresearch.org.uk/Blog/2016/11/16/john-mcdonnells-total-failure-of-an-economic-policy/

108 http://www.smf.co.uk/publications/water-nationalisation/

109   https://www.opendemocracy.net/uk/hilary-wainwright/new-economics-of-labour - scroll down for full text of speech.

the rationale for bringing back those industries into public ownership, and, crucially, the form of ownership that he wanted to promote:

> Let me be clear about this. We should not try to recreate the nationalised industries of the past.
>
> The Thatcher government and her media mouthpieces often misrepresented those nationalised industries, and ignored what they had achieved compared with the failed private companies they replaced.
>
> But we cannot be nostalgic for a model whose management was often too distant, too bureaucratic and too removed from the reality of those at the forefront of delivering services.
>
> Taking essential industries away from the whims of the market is an opportunity to move away from profit as the driver of investment and hiring decisions.
> But just as importantly it's an opportunity for us to put those industries in the hands of those who run and use them.
>
> To learn from the everyday experiences of those who know how to run railway stations, utilities and postal services, and what's needed by their users.
>
> Our socialism has never been about public ownership for the sake of it, but because we believe that nobody knows better how to run these industries than those who spend their lives with them.
> ....
> The next Labour government will put democratically owned and managed public services irreversibly in the hands of those workers, and of those who rely on their work.
>
> We will do this not only because it's right, not only because it's the most efficient way of running them, but also because the most important protection of our public services for the long term is for everyone to have and feel ownership of them.
>
> We aren't going to take control of these industries in order to put them into the hands of a remote bureaucracy, but into the hands of all of you, so that they can never again be taken away.

In other words: a fundamental shift both in the way in which these enterprises are managed as well as of ownership, on the grounds of economic necessity as well as because it is, in McDonnell's view, the right thing to do.

McDonnell argued, in a BBC Radio 4 interview, that this could be achieved through swapping government bonds for shares in a revenue-making company, and that this would be cost-free. The problem with this argument is that, quite obviously, it wouldn't be. Bonds are a form of government debt, which would add to the overall costs of servicing that debt. So, in other words, even if such a deal could be brokered there would be a long-term cost to the taxpayer.

In economic terms, clearly, that may not matter. The fact that there is a cost doesn't mean that the taxpayer is getting a bad deal. There may well be significant economic advantages; McDonnell has mentioned that the dividends paid to shareholders often outweigh profits, and a not-for-profit undertaking would not only be able to invest those dividends and profits in infrastructure, but could borrow to invest at significantly reduced interest rates (such borrowing would need to be included in the PSBR but it is possible to become too theological about such things: when the ONS determined in 2013, in response to changes in EU law on classification, that Network Rail was officially part of the public sector and its liabilities should be included in the PSBR and Net Public Debt, the additional £30bn of debt and £2.5bn on the PSBR hardly rocked the economy to its foundations, despite the claims that Ministers were making at that time about the need for austerity measures to reduce both debt and borrowing to save the economy[110]). In other words, the taxpayer could well be getting a very good deal on the back of that increased debt and borrowing. However, to claim that there is no cost to the taxpayer is, frankly, economically illiterate, in a way that undermines what is basically a wholly rational approach to taking undertakings into public ownership.

Moreover, it's an economic sleight-of-hand that is more than a little reminiscent of the Private Finance Initiative (PFI) deals that were struck in the 1990s and 2000s, in which the private sector met the up-front costs of projects while the public sector paid an annual charge, plus interest, over a period of perhaps 20-40 years. Again, the rationale was to attempt to create public assets without massive expenditure in the ~~early stages of a scheme; but while~~ committing the state to long-term payments

[110]

http://webarchive.nationalarchives.gov.uk/20160108030414/http://www.ons.gov.uk/ons/dcp171766_345415.pdf

(and also to allow what were claimed to be the superior project-management and delivery skills of the private sector to deliver schemes more efficiently – in theory, anyway). It is ironic that those on the Left who criticised PFI as an illegitimate way of taking expenditure out of the PSBR and national debt now seem to be backing a mechanism for funding nationalisation that appears to share many of the same characteristics (although John McDonnell would doubtless argue that his scheme would avoid the poor value for money that has brought PFI into disrepute)[111].

And, ultimately, the price will be determined by how highly the utility providers are able to value their future profit streams. Water and energy are highly regulated markets but the providers are operating as oligopolies in markets which are demand-inelastic I.e. demand is relatively unlikely to react to changes in price; and, being dependent on population, are likely to grow. It is difficult to see how the utilities could extract anything other than a very high long-term price for their shares. At best, the cost of that long-term commitment to the public purse is very uncertain.

Corbyn's Labour is much more radical about ownership than it is about equality – where is the evidence that this fits with popular concerns – especially since it has to develop a link between ownership and equality. This does not mean that there are not powerful arguments for public ownership – especially for activities that give rise to natural monopolies and are of crucial environmental significance. But such a policy involves trade-offs – does a nationalised water system reduce prices in the name of increasing access, or does it increase them to encourage greater long-term conservation? How does investment in, say, reservoirs mean that you avoid the disputes over where to put them. Obviously the issues aren't simple and it's intellectually dishonest to pretend that public ownership will lead us to the promised land. You need intellectual honesty. Also worth remembering the Leninist arguments about amelioration – to the extent that one genuinely wants to see a revolution happen, one should be opposed to amelioration, including the regulation of inequality through progressive taxation, welfare spending and intervention in markets. The problem remains that while Labour has always been clear on this issue, many of those around Corbyn simply aren't.

---

[111] It is perhaps ironic that one part of the UK in which PFI has not been used has been in Wales, under a Labour Government that is regarded by many of Corbyn's and McDonnell's supporters as being unacceptably centrist.

<u>Corbynism and the problem of equality</u>

One of Labour's most important economic objectives has always been the promotion of equality. But it is far from obvious that Corbyn's economic policy would achieve that; on the contrary, there is clear evidence that some of his key – and most popular – proposals would do precisely the opposite.

Take, for example, three of Corbyn's talismanic policy commitments: rail nationalisation, the abolition of tuition fees, and the abolition of parking charges at hospitals.

Renationalising the railway network is a touchstone Corbyn policy. The rationale for renationalising railway services is that the existing privatised arrangement allows train operators to extract profit from a system that ought to be operated for the public good. In pursuit of excess profit, train operators have raised the prices of services while reducing the quality of services. Superficially, there is plenty of evidence for this assertion; train services, especially on suburban commuter routes, are poor and crises – such as the adoption of new timetables in May 2018, a complete shambles which led to months of disruption, has led to a growing belief that the current railway system is not fit for purpose.

However, the reality is rather different. First, most of the railway network is already in the public sector; it is only the train operators and the rolling stock leasing companies that are in private hands. The problem is less one of ownership *per se* than the existence of a complex contractual structure that means that issues over aspects of railway operation cannot be resolved without invoking legal mechanisms – something that can only be remedied by substantial primary legislation, not by the apparently easy solution of taking franchises back into public ownership.

Second, even where a concern - be it a railway or any other type of operation – is nationalised the Government does not exercise operational control; it operates at arm's length in a way set out in statute. In the case of the old British Railways board – curiously regarded by many in Corbyn's Labour as a model for how to run a railway (which suggests that many of them are not old enough to have used its services) - the Government notoriously had almost no control over how it used the money voted for it by Parliament, exercising no more than strategic oversight.

Third, it isn't true to say that the train operating companies are extracting monopoly profit – rates of profitability in the rail industry are broadly around the average for UK industry. It is estimated that if the train operators' profits were recycled into reducing fares, the resulting fall in fares would only amount to around 4%. The real reason for soaring rail fares is the Government's quite explicit policy of reducing subsidy, and to have any impact on fares an incoming Labour government would have to decide that, among all its competing spending priorities (the NHS, collapsing local Government in England etc), increasing subsidies for rail justified a substantial shift in resources.

And, most of all, the demographic of rail users is small and predominantly privileged. According to figures published by the Department of Transport in January 2017[112], rail accounted for only 2% of all trips only 8% of the population use trains regularly; 40% of the population never use rail at all. The demographic is overwhelmingly London-centric, I.e. drawn from the wealthiest region of the UK. In 2015, people in the highest income groups made on average more than four times as many railway journeys as those in the poorest groups.

In other words, rail travel is largely an elite, London and South-East based activity. Cutting the cost of rail travel, and doing so by increasing subsidy, is essentially a bung to the affluent middle-classes – especially commuters - based on a wholly flawed analysis of the economics of rail travel. None of this is to suggest that railways should not, in principle, be in the public sector; there may well be strategic economic and environmental issues for doing so, and in economic terms the level of subsidy is, obviously, one way of reflecting the externalities. But this does imply that Corbyn Labour's rationale for renationalisation is not just based on a flawed economic analysis but that it is not, in any sense, a policy "for the many", but one that reflects the lifestyle of an affluent and London-centric Labour membership.

Similar issues are raised by the proposal to abolish tuition fees. The arguments around Labour's £11.2bn manifesto commitment to abolish fees have been well-rehearsed. On the one hand, new graduates are embarking on a career saddled by, typically, a debt £50,000; those entering socially-important professions like teaching or social work are likely never to repay that debt. And there is a more fundamental question of whether a University education is a private benefit or a public good, benefitting society as a whole; opponents of fees will argue – with

---

112

https://assets.publishing.service.gov.uk/government/uploads/system/uploads/attachment_data/file/590562/rail-passengers-factsheet-2016-revised.pdf considerable justification – that fees represent a shift from a collective to an individual view of the benefits of education.

But, once again, the evidence on who would benefit from the abolition of fees is ambiguous. Right from the outset, when the current system of fees – including the £9000 maximum – was introduced in 2010, there was significant evidence that changes to the system would ensure that the poorest students would, in the long-term, be better off; a report by the Institute of Fiscal Studies estimated that the poorest 29% would benefit[113]. And the empirical evidence – for instance, UCAS' summary of applications in 2015[114] - clearly suggests that the proportion of University applicants from disadvantaged backgrounds has increased since the new fee structure was introduced. It is reported that the abolition of tuition fees in Scotland has represented a massive middle-class subsidy, paid for by increasing debt among poorer students[115].

All of this begs the question – why tuition fees? Why did Labour commit itself to what, on its own costings, amounted to £11.2bn of priority public expenditure on a policy that gave every indication of being very far from benefitting "the many" - as distinct from, say, an increase in Sure Start and Early Years education that would benefit children from right across the economic spectrum? Once again, one speculates as to whether Corbynism was inadvertently making social policy in its own image.

There is a generational issue too. Anyone who went to University before the late 1980s (the present author included) benefitted from a free higher education, and was likely to have received a maintenance grant too (although the latter was means-tested). There is an aspect of nostalgia in all of this that needs to be addressed, and, again, one is bound to ask whether this was about the fond memories of old Lefties rather than developing a policy that fits the demands of the early-to-mid twenty-first century.

Even the popular plan to drop charges for hospital parking in England gives rise to some fundamental questions of who benefits. Nobody would seek to deny that

---

[113] https://www.ifs.org.uk/conferences/fsjune12_chowdry.pdf

[114] https://www.ucas.com/sites/default/files/january_application_rates_2015_final_0.pdf

[115] https://www.theguardian.com/education/2014/apr/29/free-tuition-scotland-benefits-wealthiest-students-most-study

abolishing the charges would be politically popular. However, there are powerful arguments that suggest that it would not be the poorest and most vulnerable who would benefit most, or even at all, from such a change. And it's one thing to say that charges need reform; another that they should be abolished entirely.

The abolition of charges in Scotland and Wales has already raised one huge problem: that car parks are so full that it is often impossible to get a space, with car-borne patients and visitors often parking in surrounding streets with all the problems that brings for local communities, who thus can be said to be bearing the costs of the policy in terms of congestion, community severance and poor air quality. But, more pertinently, the policy ignores the fact that free parking is a subsidy to the motorist, who is already likely to be among the more prosperous members of society. Department for Transport figures from 2007 show that 44% of the lowest income quintile in the UK have no access to a car, while the figure for the next-lowest quintile is around a third[116]. So it's likely to be better-off patients who will benefit from the policy, rather than the poorest and most vulnerable. (There's a further irony that a car-dependent society is leading to growing – and expensive – public health problems, with the costs falling on the NHS; encouraging further car-dependence would appear to be perverse). A genuinely redistributive policy would be looking at alternatives to car use, ensuring decent levels of access for those who do not have access to – or who would prefer not to use – a private car.

The common factor in all these policy positions is that they appear, at first sight, to benefit "the many" - but that, on closer examination, the benefits accrue most to the affluent middle classes. There is nothing new in this: there is clear evidence that this has been the general effect of apparently redistributive policies carried out by social democratic governments – including Labour governments in Britain over a long period of history and throughout Europe. There is an argument that in environments where the least well-off are also the least likely to vote, there is a political need to ensure democratic buy-in for genuinely redistributive policies.

But the point in relation to Corbynism is that, far from representing a break with traditional social democracy – let alone with traditional UK Labourism, including New Labour – what is most striking is the continuity between Corbyn's and Blair's Labour. And it is not fanciful to see this as an expression of a further continuity between Corbyn and Blair – the dominance of Party membership by those in the ABC1 socio-economic bracket, and who may well make the cognitive error of

---

[116] https://www.gov.uk/government/statistical-data-sets/nts07-car-ownership-and-access

assuming that their best interests are the same as those of society as a whole; a failure, one might suggest, of privilege-checking.

The case becomes more compelling when one considers some more general Labour policies on redistribution. The balance between tax and spending is crucial to this argument – and takes us on to territory where, for all its claims of radicalism, post-2015 Labour has been reluctant to tread.

The recent decades have seen a movement away from universal to targetted benefits. At the most superficial level of argument, universal benefits are regressive as they are received by the better-off who do not need them. But to assume that is to consider the benefits system in isolation from the way in which the money to pay those benefits is raised - I.e. through taxation.

The socialist case for universal benefits is clear; they are progressive, inclusive, cheaper to administer, and eliminate the whole bureaucracy of entitlement and enforcement. They can be offset through more progressive tax rates for higher earners[117].

However, a move back towards universal benefits still remains some way from the heart of the Corbynist project. The 2017 manifesto made welcome commitments to move away from some of the starker problems with the welfare system identified in Chapter 2 above. But the promises not to raise day-to-day spending; to stick within the Tories welfare spending framework; to freeze tax on 97% of the population all militate against that, especially when one takes into account the Institute of Fiscal Studies' warning that McDonnell's projected increases in tax revenue from corporation tax were too optimistic.

An issue that has started to gain some traction on the Left – and one that McDonnell has argued that he is open to considering – is that of a basic income[118]. [Issues of acceptability, the way in which it could work – not a radical policy on its own; something more akin to the social wage of the 1970s but actually addressing what appears to be one of the major issues facing the economy and society; the

---

[117] The case for universal benefits is set out more fully at https://policysketchbook.wordpress.com/2018/01/25/the-distributional-implications-of-universality-again/

[118] https://www.independent.co.uk/news/uk/politics/labour-universal-basic-income-john-mcdonnell-party-manifesto-corbyn-poverty-social-benefits-a8471616.html

growth of automation. Keynes and how we would only need to work a couple of hours a day, rather than the record number of hours people are working now simply to keep a roof over their head etc]

The central idea – that every citizen should receive a living income as a matter of right – is economically and politically radical; our political and social outlook is fundamentally based on the idea of wage-earning. It represents a response to a situation in which real wages have fallen, and in which, despite all the apparent benefits of automation and increasing productivity, people are on the whole working unprecedentedly long hours to earn falling real wages. "Making work pay" is the logo emblazoned on DWP offices throughout Britain; the fundamental problem is, increasingly, that it just doesn't.

Advocates of a basic income point to its inherent equality, and the fact that it would be far cheaper to administer than the existing benefits system, would ensure that there was no fraud, while ensuring that everyone had a basic standard of living[119]. It would also recognise that circumstances change, and since it would be a matter of universal entitlement there would be no place for the demonisation of the allegedly underserving - it represents a political as well as an economic statement. The evidence appears to suggest that it is affordable: of course as a society we already do pay a basic income to a very large part of the population in the form of old age pensions.

Moreover, it has the potential – in theory at least – to change the way in which we as a society view work, and for shifting the balance of reward away from the rentier class – those who make a living from exploiting assets rather than selling their labour – and thus reversing one of the major shifts of what one might call the neoliberal era.

At the same time, the idea has appealed to the economic Right – and in particular found favour with Hayek; in theory, if everyone were to receive a sufficiency, it would be possible to end support by the state for the needy, and indeed to cease provision of collective services like, for example, education and healthcare; a sufficient income would allow everyone to seek provision privately.

---

[119] A useful summary of the benefits of a universal basic income – and a plausible argument that it is wholly affordable – can be found at http://stumblingandmumbling.typepad.com/stumbling_and_mumbling/2005/04/th e_case_for_ba.html

The major argument deployed against basic income is that it rewards free riders – it allows people to expect something for nothing. Among people on the Labour Right – and not just on the right – a usual framing of Labour's position is that it is the party of work.

Australian economist Bill Mitchell explores that argument at some length a detailed blog post[120], in which he compares it with a jobs guarantee – a variant on what centre-left parties in Britain and elsewhere offer, and which was part of the programme towards which Ed Miliband appeared to be working – and argues that there is moral hazard inherent in offering a living income for nothing; although his definition of work is certainly far broader than that of the political mainstream. But there is no doubt that the idea that people are somehow getting something for nothing is deeply counter-cultural, and has become more so as the rhetoric of the deserving and undeserving poor has increasingly dominated our debate around work and social security.

It deals with the fundamental problem around the jobs guarantee that Labour offered in 2015: is that while it certainly offers a short- to medium-term fix, it does not address the fundamental problem that the state ends up paying subsidies for low pay, which, along with workfare policies (as we have seen), acts to bid down real wages[121].

But it is increasingly being argued that basic income is one response to a crisis of work in Western economies; one that both offers a challenge and an opportunity for the Left. In Britain, it is important to understand the importance of the writing of William Morris to the growth of the Labour movement. Morris' great essay *Useful Work versus Useless Toil*[122], which – coincidentally – was written during the economic crisis of the late 19th Century which austerity in the UK appears closely to resemble, contrasts the work which confers dignity and self-worth with the mechanised, alienated labour of the factory system under which the owner of capital pays the worker a price that undervalues his work – a concept that Morris of course takes straight from Marx.

---

[120] http://bilbo.economicoutlook.net/blog/?p=13025

[121] A more detailed critique of the sort of jobs guarantee that Labour was offering under Ed Miliband – and a comparison with the issues around universal basic income – can be found at http://www.coppolacomment.com/2013/07/economic-equivalence-job-guarantee-and.html

[122] https://www.marxists.org/archive/morris/works/1884/useful.htm

Morris shrewdly notices that the ideology of the dignity of work is preached most vigorously by those who do not need to work to live; that concepts of the deserving and undeserving poor are a rationalisation of the demands of capital for a cheap and obedient workforce.

And of course the assumption people need an incentive to work is both insulting and tendentious. Work – meaningful work – as Morris and others since have argued, is simply part of the human condition. The point is that the political rhetoric is based around a very narrow definition of work – namely, work that is undertaken for remuneration. There is an enormous amount of work in the broadest sense that simply does not fit into that category – one thinks immediately (and in no particular order) of internship, voluntary work, caring, parenthood, charitable fundraising, amateur dramatics, evening classes, political canvassing, blogging. All of these obviously provide value in its broadest sense, but are equally obviously not monetised; when politicians talk about "hard-working" they mean work that is paid and from which people derive a living – what a Marxist would call alienated labour. But arguably all the things I've mentioned have value; they are part of a collective process of civilised life.

And it is these things that the concept of basic income claims to liberate. Moreover, it removes – at a stroke – the coercive power of fear of losing one's living. It does not mean that essential things will not be done; but that we will have to find more co-operative ways of doing them that do not involve the coercion that comes from their being essential to putting a roof over one's head and food on the table. The call-centre of contact targets and monitored toilet breaks would be a thing of the past; as would supermarkets run on cheap workfare labour. Service industries might start offering service again. Now this is radical stuff; a system of economic activity in which labour cannot be coerced is obviously going to look very different from what we have now. But there's no evidence – none whatsoever – that the essentials would not be performed in such a society; but there is more likely to be a mature and democratic debate about what those essentials are and how they are organised. In other words, the shift of power away from rentiers and managers could be substantial. It begins to look rather like the model of worker control that John McDonnell appeared to be advocating in the more radical passages of his Alternatives to Ownership speech quoted earlier.

Utopian? Perhaps. These are big changes which fundamentally alter the power structures that support late capitalism, and it's hard to see that power being surrendered without the mother and father of fights – except that, with capitalism looking increasingly flaky and less capable by the day of providing the kind of decent living for citizens that it needs to remain stable, the political attractions of such a change may look increasingly like enlightened self-interest. And moves towards a basic income will doubtless be incremental; but as its advocates have argued, there are likely to be basic efficiencies that are achievable very quickly if we can move away from a means-tested, complicated and – yes – morally-judgmental approach to work and social security. And there is no reason why a move towards a basic income in the medium-to-long term should be incompatible with short-term policies that would bring immediate efficiencies and benefits, like a substantial increase in the minimum wage and a move towards a living wage. And in any event it seems far more rational to have a policy that's driven by a view that most people want to work and contribute than one that focusses on a small perceived problem of fecklessness, and uses that perception as a rationale for ever harsher and more damaging economic and social policies, backed up by an ever-more-complex matrix of benefits and sanctions.

Basic income on its own is not a panacea; it can become a rationale for dismantling the state and therefore moves towards a basic income must be part of a much broader political strategy. It is a policy idea that promotes vehement criticism across the political spectrum. But perhaps it will be a measure of the Corbynists seriousness of intent if serious work is undertaken to develop such an approach.

In summary, then, the economic policy developed by John McDonnell is one of the stronger parts of the Corbynist mix. McDonnell is not a man who has shied away from using some quite lurid language in the past, and his stunt of throwing the works of Chairman Mao across the despatch box at George Osborne has unfortunately outlived the point that he was seeking to make. But, in spite of that language, the policy measures that Labour is proposing are quite moderate – and that moderation may well prove to be politically awkward for a Labour government that has both raised expectations of change and has relied on attracting support from fundamentalists on the left both inside and outside the Labour Party. McDonnell may have grasped the point about the scale of the job and the need to establish priorities; there is little evidence to suggest that the Praetorian Guard of Jeremy's Twitter Army are close to doing so.

And the biggest problems appear to exist around nationalisation. The IFS has pointed out that this is the most difficult part of the Labour plan to cost; no doubt the utilities will fight tooth and nail to ensure that they extract the highest possible price. Aneurin Bevan, in founding the NHS, famously stated that in order to do it he had to stuff the consultants' mouth with gold[123]; the quantities of that gold are likely to be trivial compared with what it may take to buy out profitable utility businesses with Government bonds.

However, in stark contrast to Labour in opposition in the Miliband years, Labour is – at last – starting to ask some of the big questions: about what the economy is for, about how you address the problems of late capitalism. It is beginning to look at the questions of income, work and security – for example by examining the issues around a basic income - and is struggling towards a distinctive economic narrative, in a way that Labour has not done since the crash of 2008 rendered Blair's vision of redistribution through growth redundant. However, as writers like Paul Mason have argued, in order to get past traditional ideas of Labourism, just as likely to flourish on the Left as the Right, it's essential to move beyond some of the traditional assumptions about the dignity and utility of work. There are indications that Labour might just be starting to do that. But in order to do so, it is necessary to move beyond some basic assumptions that the Corbyn left has never shown any inclination to challenge [expand]

So, ultimately, there is a paradox. Corbyn Labour's signature policies, taken in isolation, are likely to involve the commitment of funding to boost the wellbeing of middle class people, in the most affluent parts of the UK. But the generality of policy on taxation and benefits does nothing to mitigate that redistribution, and its continuity with New Labour economics means that the aspects of the tax and benefit system that contribute most to inequality and ensure that redistribution is limited. It is ironic indeed that a party in which "Blairite" remains the choicest of insults remains, once the rhetoric is stripped away, wholly committed to a Blairite model of tax and benefits – one whose most notable characteristic is that it avoids convincing the middle classes that they need to dip into their pockets, by claiming that through top-rate tax increases, better enforcement and increases in corporation taxes, it can make fundamental changes to structures of poverty. Under Blair and Brown, while the good times lasted, the middle class did very well indeed, while, even with ameliorative measures like tax credits and Sure Start, inequality did not decrease significantly. Is that really the limit of the Corbynistas' ambition?

---

[123] https://www.independent.co.uk/life-style/health-and-families/features/the-birth-of-the-nhs-856091.html

CORBYN AND BREXIT: THE EMBEDDING OF AUSTERIAN POLITICS?

The handling of Britain's decision to leave the EU offers a telling case-study in the economics and politics of Corbyn's Labour – revealing both the ideas that motivate Corbyn and his supporters, as well as the intellectual weaknesses of their approach to economics.

The events leading up to the referendum vote to leave the EU are themselves instructive. With a few notable exceptions (of whom Corbyn was one), the Labour Party had embraced the European Union. Indeed, when Labour was in government, one of the key arguments between Tony Blair and Gordon Brown had been about whether the United Kingdom should join the Eurozone – an argument in which Brown's view that we should remain outside the Currency Union prevailed. This contrasted with Labour's historical position. In the 1980s – most notably in the 1983 General Election manifesto – Labour argued for withdrawal. Earlier, in the 1970s, Labour officially opposed the decision to join the EU in 1973, but a very substantial number of Labour MPs, led by Roy Jenkins, defied the whip to support membership. The 1975 referendum on continued membership had been a device concocted by Harold Wilson to keep the Labour Party together; in the event it produced a two-to-one majority in favour of continued membership.

The Cameron government's decision to hold a referendum was, similarly, a political fudge to keep the Conservative Party together. Europe had long been a toxic issue for the Conservative Party; it had split the Tories under John Major but Cameron was responding to the renewed rise of the Eurosceptic Right in the form of UKIP, which emerged from the 2014 European Elections as the largest single party, winning 26 seats including seven gains from Cameron's Tories[124]. The Conservatives came third in the popular vote.

Most importantly, it is necessary to consider the rise of the populist right and in particular that of UKIP, which during this period intensified its campaign for the UK to withdraw from the EU, justified on the basis of a narrative in which the UK was becoming swamped with immigrants – legal and illegal – who were taking jobs, housing and benefits from British workers while contributing nothing to the society they had moved into. It was a narrative that was exacerbated, as we saw in Chapter 2, by Labour's failure to oppose it.

Before the 2015 leadership election, Labour's clear policy was to campaign to remain in the EU.

<u>Corbyn's Euroscepticism</u>

Throughout his back-bench political career, Corbyn was a strong opponent of the EU. His rationale was closely linked to that articulated most eloquently by Tony Benn – that the EU is at its heart an organisation that entrenches capitalist values and undermines the sovereignty of Parliament, meaning that it will be impossible to deliver a transition to a Socialist society in the UK[125].

Corbyn's voting record on the EU is consistent, longstanding, clear and unequivocal:
- In the 1975 Referendum he voted against EEC membership.
- Corbyn voted against the creation of the EU in the Maastricht Treaty in 1993, speaking against it in Parliament to argue that its whole purpose was to place a committee of bankers at the heart of EU policy-making, to ensure price stability and therefore a neoliberal set of values.
- Corbyn voted against the Lisbon treaty in 2008;
- Corbyn has consistently voted against EU-related measures in Parliament, including in 2011 on the creation of the European Stability Mechanism, designed to assist poorer EU Member States; and against UK participation in the EU Banking Authority in 2012.

124

https://en.wikipedia.org/wiki/European_Parliament_election,_2014_(United_King dom)

[125] Extracts from the relevant speeches can be found at https://web.archive.org/web/20180107195608/http://www.leftleave.org/jeremy-corbyn-on-the-european-union/

- During his leadership campaign in 2015, Corbyn stated that he would not rule out campaigning for a vote to leave, in response to the Government's position on workers' rights[126]

In each case Corbyn made common cause with Eurosceptic MPs on the hard Right of the Conservative Party. But, more importantly, this has been a mainstream view of the EU on the Left – especially on the non-Labour left[127]. In particular, the issue of Parliamentary sovereignty allowed such unlikely combinations of politicians as Enoch Powell and Tony Benn to make common cause over the decades of debate about the EU.

Most parties on the non-Labour Left – including Respect, the Communist Party, the Socialist Labour Party, and the Trade Union and Socialist Coalition (TUSC) whose members include the Socialist Party – chose to support leaving the EU in the Referendum[128]. Their belief – along with some in the Labour Party – is that the EU is a fundamentally undemocratic organization which aims to embed what they regard as "neoliberal" values of privatization, free markets and free trade. They point to the the EU's response to the Greek financial crisis – in which creditor nations imposed a programme of intense cuts and austerity on the Greek state – as an example of this.

But there is another story. Under the Presidency of Jacques Delors from 1985-1995, the EU sought to promote the European Social Model[129] promoting what were described as fundamental social rights, social protection through welfare programmes and redistributive policies, the right to collective bargaining, and state responsibility for full employment – to the frustration of Margaret Thatcher, among

---

[126] http://blogs.lse.ac.uk/brexit/2015/12/07/the-labour-partys-european-policy-under-jeremy-corbyn-no-brexit-no-grexit/

[127] See, for example, Socialist Worker's coverage of the launch of the Left Leave campaign:
https://socialistworker.co.uk/art/42550/Launch+of+united+left+campaign+to+leave+the+EU

[128]
https://en.wikipedia.org/wiki/United_Kingdom_European_Union_membership_referendum,_2016#Party_policies

[129] https://www.etuc.org/en/european-social-model

others. As recently as 2007 the European Socialist Parties were promoting the importance of maintaining the Social Model, without any doubt that the institutions of the EU were, in principle, capable of doing so[130]. In fact the EU Treaties are drawn in a way that can admit a range of interpretations, and the political emphasis of the Union has changed over time – often as a result of the leadership of Member States building consensus behind policy positions.

<u>Referendum campaign</u>

Unsurprisingly, given his background, Corbyn's contribution to the 2016 Referendum campaign was widely criticised for being half-hearted and inept. Famously, Corbyn went on holiday for a week at a key stage in the campaign; and both he and those around him were widely accused of sabotaging the Labour campaign against Brexit – for example by removing pro-European lines from Shadow Ministerial speeches. When he was asked on a Channel Four chat show how he would rate the EU out of ten, he notoriously offered a modest seven to seven-and-a-half[131]; hardly the endorsement of a leader seriously engaged in the campaign.

Corbyn and Labour were largely invisible during the campaign – research by Loughborough University showed that at the peak of the referendum campaign, Labour voices were present in around 4% of broadcast media coverage and 8% of print media coverage of the campaign[132], attributing this in part to Corbyn's refusal to appear on cross-party platforms. Even when Corbyn did enter the debate, it was to criticise the EU and press the case for reform, rather than offer it support.

Having attended the Labour campaign launch in Cardiff, it might be worth my presenting some personal reflections on what that event demonstrated about Corbyn's view on Brexit. The event, in Cardiff City Hall, was supposed to bring together Corbyn and Shadow Chancellor John McDonnell, who, in the event, failed to show and was replaced by Owen Smith (at that stage still a member of the Shadow Cabinet).

---

[130]   https://www.pes.eu/export/sites/default/.galleries/Documents-gallery/Old-documents/new_social_europe_web_en.pdf_2063069339.pdf

[131]   https://www.bbc.co.uk/news/av/uk-politics-eu-referendum-36506163/corbyn-i-m-seven-out-of-10-on-eu

[132]   http://blog.lboro.ac.uk/crcc/eu-referendum/report-finds-labour-almost-invisible-eu-referendum-coverage/

The difference between Corbyn and Smith was striking. Smith was passionate and chose to discuss the original thinking behind the European Union – the need to secure peace and prosperity across a continent that had been ravaged by war and, in the 1930s, catastrophic economic depression. Corbyn, on the other hand, ratlled through his speech, reading out an obviously-prepared text without showing any evidence of commitment (it is one of Corbyn's weaknesses as a speaker – and perhaps an indication of of his inexperience of office or Government – that it is always obvious when he is not really personally committed to a political position). Meanwhile, a clutch of Corbyn aides whose job was apparently to check the speech against delivery loitered and sniggered at the side of the hall. There was no pretence at engagement.

Leaving aside the questions of Corbyn's personal commitment, it was notable that, during a campaign in which the Leave side was consistently expressing big themes like national sovereignty, control over the UK's future destiny, and its views on immigration, Corbyn consistently resorted to esoterica rather than pressing the mainstream economic case for remaining – which is that EU withdrawal would be an economic disaster whose brunt would be borne most heavily by those who were already the poorest and most vulnerable in society. For example, he referred instead to the Transatlantic Trade and Investment Partnership (TTIP)[133] – which by nid 2016 was already effectively dead[134] - or the Posted Workers' Directive[135] – an obscure piece of EU legislation that nobody had heard of and whose effect was, frankly, minimal.

Perhaps the greatest moment of sheer embarrasment of Corbyn's referendum campaign – the one that revealed his refusal to engage with, and inability to understand, the key issues – came the morning after the referendum, when he

[133]   https://www.independent.co.uk/voices/comment/what-is-ttip-and-six-reasons-why-the-answer-should-scare-you-9779688.html

[134] https://www.telegraph.co.uk/business/2016/08/28/eus-ttip-trade-deal-with-the-us-has-collapsed-says-germany/

[135] I explain the detail of the directive – and why it is irrelevant to the debate – at https://notesbrokensociety.wordpress.com/2018/03/12/the-posted-workers-directive-is-an-excuse-not-a-reason-for-opposing-the-single-market/

[136] https://labourlist.org/2016/06/corbyn-article-50-has-to-be-invoked-now/ It is interesting, and profoundly relevant to the issues around Corbyn and the cult of personality, that it was quite commonplace for his supporters to argue later on social media that he had said no such thing.

called for the Government to trigger Article 50 of the TFEU, setting in motion immediately the timetable for withdrawal[136]. In the event the Government waited nine months before doing so, and in the intervening period has proved itself completely incapable of developing an intelligible negotiating position and hence of engaging in meaningful negotiations. How much less possible would this have been if the two-year deadline had been triggered the morning after? It was a moment in which Corbyn demonstrated his wholescale ignorance of how the institutions of Government work, and of the kind of processes that are necessary to deliver policy.

In the event, the issue that dominated the EU referendum campaign was immigration – an issue on which, as we saw in Chapter 2, Labour has long been deeply conflicted. In the event, Labour's referendum position was simply to reject the case for freedom of movement; in other words, Labour completely accepted and legitimised the framing of the debate adopted by UKIP and the Eurosceptic Tory Right. In other words, confronted with an issue both of principle and fact, a Labour leadership that had adopted the motto "straight talking, honest politics" was capable of neither.

Since the Referendum, the Conservative Government – again, one suspects, responding to the need to keep a fissiparous party together – has made it clear that it intends to push for a Brexit that takes the UK out of the Customs Union and the Single Market altogether – in stark contrast to the commitments given by prominent Conservative Brexit supporters that the UK could and should remain within these institutions once it left.

The rationale for this position is based squarely on the referendum result: Britain voted to leave, and to take back control to Parliament; that means it must be outside institutions that have the power to set rules, and outside the jurisdiction of the European Court (although that position appears to have been modified to the limited extent that realism has set in).

<u>Since the Referendum</u>

The Labour leadership's position on the EU has, since the referendum, been to accept the outcome; to prepare for Brexit and to secure a deal that protects British jobs, but rejects the existing single market and Customs Union structures on the grounds that they would leave Britain as a "rule-taker" - while arguing the case for "a" customs union to ensure frictionless cross-border trade. Labour's EU spokesman, Sir Keir Starmer MP, has consistently argued that the reasons for the vote to leave the EU – especially in the economically and socially-less favoured areas of the UK outside London and the South East – represented a rejection of the political system that the political class must listen to and respect.

Labour's main policy statement, set out by its Brexit spokesman, Keir Starmer[137], has been that any deal between the UK and the EU must meet six tests:

* Does it ensure a strong and collaborative future relationship with the EU?
* Does it deliver the "exact same benefits" as we currently have as members of the Single Market and Customs Union?
* Does it ensure the fair management of migration in the interests of the economy and communities?
* Does it defend rights and protections and prevent a race to the bottom?
* Does it protect national security and our capacity to tackle cross-border crime?
* Does it deliver for all regions and nations of the UK?

Starmer has given a commitment that there must be a meaningful vote in Parliament on the final deal, and Labour will oppose any deal that does not meet these criteria. However, the six points are problematic. The second, in particular, led to a somewhat unseemly response from Labour's International Trade spokesman Barry Gardiner MP, who notoriously described it as "bollocks"[138]. His argument – with which it is difficult to disagree – is that the only way in which you can have "the exact same" benefits as the UK's current EU membership is to retain that membership; and in doing so points out that rather than repeating this Conservative commitment, Labour should instead have held them to account over it.

But, leaving aside the inelegance of expression, the point remains that effectively Labour's policy is ambiguous. The Labour leadership talks of "a" Customs Union and "a" Single Market that differs from the existing relationship insofar as it protects workers' rights and allows the UK to strike its own trade deals outside the EU framework[139]. In other words, there is at the heart of the Labour Party's policy on

---

137 https://labourlist.org/2017/03/keir-starmer-labour-has-six-tests-for-brexit-if-theyre-not-met-we-wont-back-the-final-deal-in-parliament/

138   https://www.theguardian.com/politics/2018/apr/10/labour-minister-barry-gardiner-sorry-good-friday-agreement-shibboleth

139   https://www.theguardian.com/politics/2018/jun/05/labour-reveals-scheme-to-maintain-access-to-eu-single-market

this crucial issue a fundamental ambiguity; one that appears to be founded in exactly the same mindset of the Government that you can cherry-pick the bits of EU membership that you like and strike a deal to avoid the others – commonly known as "cakeism". The problem is that the EU negotiators have said that this kind of deal simply isn't available; it's not just illogical, it's never going to be on the table. The EU has said, in terms, that it's just not going to allow a departing UK to pick and choose which bits of the Treaty obligations it likes, least of all when they concern the four pillars of the EU treaties.

The conclusion on this issue is not that Labour is playing a "long game", as Corbyn's supporters claim, or least of all a clever one. It is acting within exactly the same framing of the issues as the Government, and it has neither grasped the nature of the EU institutions or the likely scope of the negotiations (and, above all, that the UK is in these negotiations a supplicant, dealing with a much stronger economic power that has nothing like the UK's stake in ensuring that the negotiations succeed). It is all of a piece with the trademark Corbynist technique of focussing on headlines, not details, and of developing positions to appeal to its supporters rather than working towards outcomes.

The Starmer position on respecting the vote has been backed by a number of MPs for predominantly Northern constituencies who have argued that Labour cannot contradict what they regard as the "authentically working class" nature of the vote to Leave. These MPs include long-term opponents of the EU like Frank Field MP but also people like Caroline Flint MP, more usually associated with the Labour Party's Progress wing. But this position is problematic at a number of levels.

First, it appears not to be true. It appears not to be the case that the vote to leave was dominated by those who had been left behind. Research undertaken at Leicester University appears to show that the real reasons for the leave vote were cultural rather than economic; that the vote to leave was swung by white, older, home-owning, affluent people with comfortable pensions; people who felt the erosion of the entitlement they had previously enjoyed – and the very people who were least likely to vote for a Labour Party led by Jeremy Corbyn[140].

Second, almost every piece of research done on the attitudes of Labour Party members show that they overwhelmingly oppose Brexit and would support a vote on

---

[140]   I   have   summarised   the   research   at https://notesbrokensociety.wordpress.com/2018/02/23/new-evidence-shows-that-the-brexit-vote-was-not-the-revolt-of-the-left-behind-will-labour-respond/

the outcome of the deal – something that, with a few exceptions, the leadership of the Labour Party opposes[141].

Third, there is now growing evidence from polls – most recently a major poll undertaken for Hope Not Hate and published at length in the Observer[142] - that those areas are swinging against Brexit as the consequences become clear; as the debate moves from the reified world of "taking back control" or abstract discussions about immigrations or bogus numbers on the sides of buses, and people are confronted with the likely consequences of Brexit, soft or hard – and the Government's apparent failure to get any kind of grip on the negotiations[143].

Finally, there remains a question – one that goes to the heart of the Corbyn project in many ways – of what MPs are *for*. There is a small group of Labour MPs who have long opposed the EU and their position is at least consistent. But for others, there appears to be a conflict in which they are using the vote in their constitutencies in order to rationalize continued support for a process which they do not believe is in the best interests of their constituents – and which they understand to be damaging. And, paradoxically, that is presented as a gesture of *respect* for their constituents.

And that is the paradox that arises when a simplistic view of political mandates – based in turn on the vanguard theory of political parties – comes up against the real world of changing circumstances and changing minds. It reflects the leadership position that Labour must respect the referendum vote, which is fine as far as it goes. But the question that one must ask – both of the Labour MPs who continue to back a more complete form of Brexit than even Corbyn advocates, by, for example, arguing against staying in the Single Market – and of the Labour leadership's position, is simply this: which is more respectful, to stand up and fight for what you believe to be best for your constituents – or even your country – or to walk away in the face of a one-off vote, especially when it becomes apparent that opinion is changing?

---

[141] This research is typical – although now a few months old: https://labourlist.org/2018/01/labour-members-poll-over-75-per-cent-of-want-vote-on-brexit-deal-and-to-stay-in-single-market-and-customs-union/

[142] https://www.theguardian.com/politics/2018/aug/11/more-than-100-pro-leave-constituencies-switch-to-remain

[143] https://www.theguardian.com/politics/2018/aug/11/brexit-swansea-leave-voting-turns-against-brexit-remain

<u>Corbyn and the Brexit process</u>

Corbyn has made a number of speeches on the post-Brexit economy that show a deep and fundamental inability to understand the issues around international trade – and which raise questions about Corbyn's credentials as an internationalist. And he has continued to argue that EU rules would prevent a Labour government from delivering its programme in office.

Two speeches in particular demonstrate the problems with Corbyn's approach to the EU – the wilful lack of understanding and his willingness to indulge in crude economic generalisations that misunderstand the nature of immigration and competition.

The first of these was a speech to the Scottish Labour Party conference in March 2018[144]. It displayed an approach to the EU that was mired in both ignorance and casual racism. The offending passage read as follows:

> "We cannot be held back inside or outside the EU from taking the steps we need to develop and invest in cutting edge industries and local business stop the tide of privatisation and outsourcing, or from preventing employers being able to import cheap agency labour to undercut existing pay and conditions in the name of free market orthodoxy.

> It's striking that Theresa May's only clear priority when she laid out her new Brexit negotiating position last week seemed to be to tie the UK permanently to EU rules, which are used to drive privatisation and block support for British industry.

> The European Union is set to make changes of its own in the coming period especially in relation to the rules governing Eurozone economies and the rights of temporary migrant workers.

> It would therefore be wrong to sign up to a single market deal without agreement that our final relationship with the EU would be fully compatible with our radical plans to change Britain's economy.

[144]   https://labourlist.org/2018/03/labour-in-scotland-is-back-corbyns-full-speech-to-scottish-conference/

We are determined to negotiate a deal that gives us full tariff-free access to the single market.

But if we are genuinely going to have a jobs first Brexit that deal must be compatible with our plans to bring the railways and postal service into full public ownership transform energy markets and end the privatisation of our public services.

And we also need to be clear we could not accept a situation where we were subject to all EU rules and EU law, yet had no say in making those laws That would leave us as mere rule-takers and isn't a tenable position for a democracy."

The narrative is obvious: a claim that the EU's institutions would prevent Labour from enacting its economic programme and would allow immigration that would reduce the wages of British workers."

But neither statement withstands scrutiny.

On the first point, far from preventing Member States' governments from taking industries into private ownership and retaining them there, the EU Treaties do precisely the opposite: Article 345 of the Treaty on the Functioning of the Europan Union explicitly states that Member States have the right to decide over the balance between public and private ownership[145].

Second, the rules on State Aids and procurement state, respectively, that Member States should not use subsidy to undermine the operation of the single market (and contain explicit provisions that allow Member States to be exempted in cases where to do so would promote other EU aims such as regional development, technical innovation, promotion of small and medium enterprises and environmental protection)[146]; and, in the case of procurement, govern the process for outsourcing in the event that a Member State decides to do so in line with the principle of subsidiarity, which rules that economic (and other) decisions should be delegated down to the most appropriate political level.

---

[145] https://eur-lex.europa.eu/legal-content/EN/ALL/?uri=CELEX%3A12008E345

[146] http://europa.eu/rapid/press-release_MEMO-17-1342_en.htm

It is a truism that the EU Treaties have free movement of people, goods, service and capital as their absolute and fundamental principle; but none of this – none whatsoever[147] – prevents Labour from delivering its programme. There's nothing new or controversial about any of this; and it difficult to see how an intellectually honest Labour leader, in the face of all the evidence[148], could continue pushing this line.

And, alongside this, Corbyn continues to push the utterly discredited line that immigration has reduced the wages of UK workers. The evidence has always shown that immigration is good for the economy and actually drives up wages; it is an engine of growth and prosperity[149].

Moreover there is emerging evidence[150] that any post-Brexit restriction of immigration will damage the economy – and hence the living standards of working people – at least as much as the damage to trade. But the Labour Party – Right and Left - has always had a problem with this issue – as noted in the discussion in Chapter 2 of the anti-immigration mugs that Labour HQ saw fit to distribute at the 2015 election, to the fury of many within the wider Party. There has traditionally been a line on the Labour Right that we need an "honest" debate about immigration; but that has usually meant a dishonest debate in which Labour patronises its supporters by privileging doorstep prejudice over hard economic evidence, and in which excuses are found not to challenge the Tory framing of the issue.

---

[147] See, for example https://www.anothereurope.org/wp-content/uploads/2018/03/aeip-reform-final-web.pdf which fact-checks the claim that the EU prevents Labour from delivering its programme.

[148] Much of which can be found here: http://renewal.org.uk/blog/eu-law-is-no-barrier-to-labours-economic-programme

[149] See, for example, this paper compiled for the UK Home Office in 2001 https://mpra.ub.uni-muenchen.de/75900/ or, more recently, a video from NIESR in which Jonathan Portes summarises the evidence https://www.niesr.ac.uk/blog/impacts-immigration-niesr-director-jonathan-portes-summarises-evidence-video#.V11JRDUsrGs

[150] See, for example, https://voxeu.org/article/economic-impact-brexit-induced-reductions-migration-uk

In the second speech, billed as the start of Labour's "Build it in Britain Again" campaign[151], delivered on 24 July 2018, Corbyn's position had moved on – partly perhaps in response to the Tory Party's disarray – but still contains deep and fundamental misunderstandings about international trade and what the EU does.

Corbyn's basic argument is that the UK needs to take advantage of what he regards as a key benefit of Brexit – the fall in the value of the pound – to reboot investment in the UK's manufacturing industry, to regain jobs that had been lost abroad owing to what Corbyn described as "a kind of magical thinking" that emphasised jobs in services – and especially the financial sector – above manufacturing, while allowing goods produced by cheap labour abroad

It's a speech that shows profound ignorance of the dynamics of trade and investment. Just to take a few examples:

- a low Pound makes imports more expensive, as well as exports cheaper. A large proportion of the raw materials used by industry are imported. So, obviously, costs and prices will rise.

- as anyone who has followed the Brexit debate knows, most manufacturing supply chains cross borders - and do so because it is more economically-efficient, offsetting the costs of physically moving goods. A huge proportion of UK trade is in unfinished, not finished goods. But in a post-Brexit world, how will a British industry which does not have the advantage of frictionless trade in partially-finished goods compete with places that do - especially when you factor in the cost of tariffs and border delays?

- the low pound also impacts food prices - obviously, since only 40% of our food is grown in the UK. Increasing food prices means lower disposable household incomes. So how is demand for the British goods going to be maintained in a shrinking domestic market?

- in a post-Brexit world - with the likely effect on GDP - where is the investment in manufacturing going to come from? Public expenditure from a reduced public purse, crowding out resources for health, education etc? A huge proportion of manufacturing investment in the UK - which, admittedly, is too low at the moment - comes from inward investment by

---

[151]   https://labourlist.org/2018/07/build-it-in-britain-again-corbyns-full-speech/

businesses seeking access to the single market. How is that going to be replaced? Nye Bevan wrote that the language of priorities is the religion of Socialism - Corbyn appears not to have a basic understanding about any of this.

- ultimately it is just not possible to compete on price with goods with lower input costs. The only way is to cut those costs - which means more automation, which means fundamental changes to employment patterns. Do we really think that a diminished and isolated Britain will be able to manage those long-term changes in the nature of employment and work on its own? In 2018, are we really supposed to believe that Socialism in One Country is an intelligent economic option?

But it is worth noting that, yet again, and as noted in the previous chapter, the common theme is that the most important economic issues are not growth, productivity, employment or even equality – but *ownership*. Yet again, Labour's discussion of economic issues is marred by its inability to move beyond this particular comfort zone. But Corbyn's rhetoric is also based on a nostalgic and outmoded view of the workplace – a view of factories and production lines that is no longer relevant to the British economy, where manufacturing is more likely to be technologically-advanced and structured in an entirely different way[152]. It is interesting that one of the most trenchant critics of founding left politics on the old-style industrial model is Corbyn-supporting Paul Mason, whose *Postcapitalism* argues[153] that the left has to respond to precisely those changes that Corbyn appears incapable of recognising. And his apparent inability to understand that, in a modern industrial economy, supply chains cross borders is a clear indication of the shallowness of Corbyn's economic knowledge; it increases the concern that Corbyn is not interested in understanding, or opening a dialogue with, the business sector.

---

[152] One of the more telling moments of Corbyn's first leadership campaign came when he suggested that the South Wales coal mines might be re-opened. As a political idea this was never a runner; leaving aside the fact that coal-burning for power is deeply environmentally damaging, it was pointed out at the time that only a privileged Londoner, brought up on Labour mythology, could suggest that such a policy that looked backward rather than forward, and involving back-breaking and dangerous work, was appropriate in the early 21st century: https://www.mirror.co.uk/news/uk-news/jeremy-corbyn-could-bring-back-6213691

[153] Mason *Postcapitalism* (2015): London, Allen Lane

At the time of writing (August 2018), with the Government in disarray over Brexit, and with the European Commission negotiator having dismissed Theresa May's carefully crafted Cabinet compromise negotiating position as unacceptable, it is difficult to see where the Labour party will go. Pressure is mounting for a second referendum – or at the very least a popular vote on the deal – while the public debate is increasingly focussed around the catastrophe of leaving the EU without a deal. There is talk of Government stockpiling food and medicines as the UK ports seize up. Corbyn's express remains that there is no need for a second referendum, and that Labour, if it won a General Election, would negotiate a "jobs first" Brexit. But that line is looking increasingly untenable, and there appear to be signs that the Labour Party is at least contemplating the possibility of a popular vote on any deal that Theresa May can agree.

<u>Brexit as culture war</u>

As the above has shown, the Labour leadership has shown a consistent inability to understand the institutions of the EU, and the economics of withdrawal. But there is a further failure, drawing both on Labour's ambiguity over the vote and, it could be argued, on the nature of Labour's new membership itself. And that is the failure to understand Brexit as part of a longer-term culture war, and as the culmination of a right-wing project that goes right back to Thatcher. Some Labour critics of Brexit have understood this[154]; the leadership simply has not engaged with this aspect of Brexit.

There is no doubt that, since the referendum vote, the atmosphere of politics in the UK has changed fundamentally – the political expression of questions like nationalism and race has become less inhibited. It has been an environment in which, as we have seen, the alt-Right has thrived; one in which reified concepts of sovereignty and control have come to dominate political discourse. As I argued earlier, the nature of the Corbyn Labour Party's mass membership makes it deeply susceptible to reification, and thus it lacks the ability to make empirical and rational arguments; [this needs a lot of expansion]

In summary, then, Corbyn's Labour's position over the EU has appeared conflicted and shambolic. Labour's performance in the EU referendum was poor – its near-invisibility partly due to the media's portrayal of the EU issue as being an

---

[154] I heard Andrew Adonis making precisely this point about Brexit as the culmination of the Thatcher project at a meeting in Aberdare in May 2018 – part of his tour around the UK to Brexit-voting areas.

internal Tory Party fight, but largely down to Corbyn's - and his political allies' - Euroscepticism and lack of enthusiasm for the cause.   There was no leadership whatsoever.

After the referendum the Labour Party was faced with a choice – of acquiescing in the Tory framing of the result as "the will of the people" (this of course preceded the growing awareness of the corruption inherent in the conduct of the Leave campaign), or of standing up for what, deep down, it knows to be in the best interests of the people for whom Labour speaks – which is to stay in the EU. The fact that many of the most deprived areas of the UK voted to leave does not change the fact that on every credible analysis it is those areas which will be hit hardest by Brexit. It had the opportunity to oppose the choices that Theresa May made – not in the national interest, but in the interests of keeping her divided party together, just as David Cameron had done in holding the referendum – but did not do so, mesmerised by that vote. It consistently refused to speak up for the benefits of freedom of movement within Europe, and to speak for the millions of EU citizens who have made their home in the EU.

In other words, the policy followed by Labour on Brexit has not been bold, or radical – and certainly not "for the many". It represents the sort of triangulated fudge that one would normally associate with New Labour; and is replete with the irony of wholly accepting Tory framing on an issue on which Tony Blair – and many of those associated with him, like Andrew Adonis – have taken a clear stand. There is a deeply unpalatable irony in the fact that among Corbyn supporters, "Blairite" is the usual insult of choice directed at those who challenge their world view, and yet Corbyn's position on Europe, as Brexit has unfolded, has given every appearance of being a caricature of the worst things of which Blair was accused – the acceptance of neoliberal framing, the acceptance of an elite Thatcherite project, and a determination to fudge this away by a form of triangulation.

LABOUR AND ANTISEMITISM

Of all the issues that have been raised concerning Jeremy Corbyn's Labour, the accusation that it is institutionally antisemitic has been one of the most damaging and persistent. It is important because, whether one agrees with the proposition or not, it raises some fairly fundamental questions about both the theoretical and practical aspects of Corbyn's Labour Party[155].

The accusation matters because it goes to the heart of what Corbyn and his party is supposed to represent. Corbyn has been represented as an unswerving campaigner against racism in all its forms – a claim that forms part of the central narrative that he has been a fearless campaigner whose personal integrity is beyond reproach in a deeply corrupt and compromised political system; and one who has in particular offered consistent and unstinting support for the Palestinian cause in the face of oppression by the Israeli government. Corbyn's supporters will frequently claim that antisemitism has frequently been used to shield the Israeli government from legitimate criticism of its treatment of Palestinians. And, more generally, that anti-racism is at the heart of Corbynism and the ethos of his supporters.

Against this, there are consistent accusations that Corbyn has consistently shared platforms with antisemites and Holocaust deniers, and with people who deny the right of the state of Israel to exist; that he worked for the state TV of Iran, an antisemitic state; and that people on the Corbynist wing of the Labour party have been allowed to express antisemitic views, including Holocaust denial, on social media in particular without any effective sanction from the Party hierarchy.

---

[155] It is important to bear in mind that, at the time of writing, the issues surrounding allegations of antisemitism in the Labour Party are far from resolved. This chapter will therefore focus on a discussion of the background to the Corbynist Labour position, rather than offering a detailed discussion of the specific issues.

There are therefore two levels of accusation. The first is that Corbyn is himself an antisemite, who has been quite happy to ally himself personally with – and appear on platforms alongside - people who preach antisemitism and even Holocaust denial; and who has persistently failed to condemn antisemitism as a form of racism, using the evasive phrase that he is opposed to all forms of racism and discrimination. Those who take this view point to his refusal to appear on the same platform as Tony Blair during the 2016 EU referendum as an example of an obvious double-standard.

The second is that Corbyn's leadership has seen an environment created in the Labour Party in which antisemitism – in particular an antisemitism related to hostility to the existence of the state of Israel – has been allowed to flourish, and indeed has become one of the political factors that unites the people who run the Labour Party.

While in recent times – and in particular since the Second World War - antisemitism has long been associated with the political far right, it has a long tradition on the left, dating right back to the middle of the nineteenth century. More recently, however, antisemitism became one of the staples, for example, of Communist ideology in the Soviet Bloc, most notably under Stalin, but also revived in the 1970s[156].

To understand this one needs to consider the writing of Moishe Postone, the recently-deceased Marxist academic who examined what he called structural antisemitism on the Left. To put it briefly, this structural antisemitism relies on a simplistic view of Jews as part of the structures of power around capitalism; as the only minority that has been on the side of capitalist power. The relationship between Jews and power has been a complex one, as writers like Hannah Arendt have pointed out, but in the world of simplistic Leftism that nuance has been lost; Jewish financiers are seen as part of the structure of capitalism (as it happens missing the key Marxist point that capitalism is about structures, not individuals). Thus, attacking Jews, and Jewish institutions, becomes bound up with being an anti-capitalist. Postone described the racism of antisemitism as "pseudo-emancipatory";

---

[156] An exhaustive view of Stalisinism and antisemitism can be found at https://www.workersliberty.org/story/2017-07-26/stalinist-roots-left-anti-semitism-0, although it is important to understand that this comes from the Alliance for Workers' Liberty, an ultra-Trotskyite grouping that is currently on the Labour Party's prohibited list.

it pretends to strike at power while actually reinforcing it. It is, at heart, a symptom of crude thinking – or an absence of thinking; Postone himself argued that the elimination of antisemitism – and the intellectual errors that somehow see it as part of the Left's critique of capital – was an essential task for the Left.

More recently, writers like Daniel Allington and David Hirsch have examined the roots and practices of left antisemitism. Allington points out to key characteristics of antisemitism, and how it differs from other forms of racism; while racist discourse usuallly argues that the subjects of racism are essentially inferior – either genetically or culturally – antisemitism is based on the illicit power allegedly exercised by Jews; the classic text of modern antisemitism is The Protocols of the Elders of Zion, the notorious forgery that describes a Jewish conspiracy to control the world. (The antisemitism that defined Nazi rule in Germany of course used both narratives).

In recent years, the resurgence of antisemitism on the left can be closely linked to the issue of Palestine. In an age when - as Hirsch has argued – the key narrative on the left has been "anti-imperialism", combined with opposition to colonialism and racism, Left antisemitism has positioned itself in opposition to what it claims is the Jewish role in the world order, with the state of Israel as a key player in the current Western domination of the world. The question of the Israeli state's relation to Palestinians has therefore become something much more than a conventional question about how a government has treated a minority within its borders; the existence of the state of Israel itself has become a central point of debate. One element of that debate has been to question aspects of, or even the veracity of the Holocaust – for example, when former Labour politician Ken Livingstone[157] tried to revive the long-discredited[158] myth that Hitler had in effect supported Zionism, through his signature of the Haavara agreement which purported to allow some German Jews to emigrate to Palestine.

However, Allington argues in his review of antisemitic statements on social media that many of the older antisemitic tropes – such as the blood libel[159] and the

---

[157]   https://www.theguardian.com/politics/2017/mar/30/ken-livingstone-repeats-claim-nazi-zionist-collaboration

[158] **See, for example** https://theconversation.com/labour-antisemitism-row-there-was-nothing-zionist-about-hitlers-plans-for-the-jews-58656

[159] https://en.wikipedia.org/wiki/Blood_libel

conspiracy theory – have become standards of modern antisemitism, in which the terms "Jew" and "Israeli" have become increasingly interchangeable.

In his review of antisemitic postings on social media – concentrating on three pro-Corbyn groups on Facebook, Allington describes three principal narratives at the heart of pro-Corbyn antisemitic discourse:

- First, what David Hirsch has called "The Livingstone Formulation[160]" – that reference to antisemitism is an attempt to stifle free speech on the subject of Israel on the left. The Livingstone Formulation, according to Hirsch, is essentially a methodology for refusing to engage with accusations of antisemitism – it starts with a refusal to discuss the substance of an allegation by questioning motive, moving on to a counter- accusation that the questioner is making a false statement; and then to conflate the antisemitic statement into a single category of statements which are characterised as "criticism"; and finally accusing the questioner of using the accusation as part of a conspiracy to silence this "criticism". Hirsch argues that this accusation is often accompanied by a statement of the respondent's own history of opposition to all forms of racism.

- Second, outright denial – a refusal to accept that there is antisemitism in the Labour Party, or to dismiss the issue as part of a plot to discredit Corbyn and his supporters (normally accompanied by the claim that Corbyn has spent his life fighting against racism and discrimination of all kinds).

- Third, arguments from collective responsibility: the claim that because historically some Jews have behaved in a certain way, that behaviour represents a racial trait; what Allington calls the "some Jews" repertory. Obviously, that represents a deeply antisemitic form of expression, and is often bound up with conspiracy theory.

In general, though, it is clear that there is a profoundly antisemitic discourse that flourishes among individuals and groups, and that this is not only tolerated by many people in the Labour Party but, insofar as they believe that this antisemitic discourse

---

160   https://engageonline.wordpress.com/2016/04/29/the-livingstone-formulation-david-hirsh-2/

is about the defence of the Palestinian people, is at the heart of the political beliefs of those Labour (and Corbyn) supporters.

Discussion of the Livingstone Formulation inevitably brings to mind Jeremy Corbyn's claim – and the claim made on his behalf by his supporters – that he has been a lifelong opponent of all forms of racism; a claim that is frequently made on his behalf by his supporters on social media.   I see little doubt that Corbyn sincerely *thinks* he is anti-racist, and that his supporters do so too. Where that claim becomes problematic is the context, and the apparent inability of the Left – partly influenced by that intellectual background of anti-imperialism – to get to grips with antisemitism as racism, and to separate it from formulations about Zionism.

An example is the case of Corbyn's opposition to the removal of what was a very obviously antisemitic mural in Tower Hamlets – a story that was extensively covered in the media at the time[161]. The criticism at the time was not so much that Corbyn was celebrating antisemitism as such (although that accusation was made), but that he lacked the contextual framework to recognise how offensive the mural was – especially when one adds to the mural itself the painter's comments about "Rothschilds and Warburgs", invoking familiar antisemitic tropes about conspiracy and world domination.

<u>Labour and the IHRA definition of antisemitism</u>

The argument within the Labour Party has become crystallised around the controversy as to whether to adopt in full the working definition of antisemitism developed by the International Holocaust Remembrance Alliance (IHRA)[162] – including the supporting examples – as the basis for its definition of antisemitism in the party's rules. The definition has been accepted in its entirety by all the Governments of the member nations of the UK (including the Labour Government in Wales[163]) and by public bodies in the UK including the Crown Prosecution Service, as a basis for assessing grounds for prosecution[164].

---

[161]   https://www.theguardian.com/commentisfree/2018/mar/28/antisemitism-open-your-eyes-jeremy-corbyn-labour

[162]   https://www.holocaustremembrance.com/working-definition-antisemitism?usergroup=5

[163]
https://gov.wales/about/cabinet/cabinetstatements/2017/definitionantisemitism/?lang=en

It's not necessary to go into the twist and turns of the issues around the adoption of this definition. The key point is the way in which, through all those twists and turns, the Labour hierarchy has believed that it knows better than the representatives of the Jewish community what antisemitism looks like – in particular in the arguments over the examples of antisemitism that form part of the IHRA definition, but are essentially there to provide context and examples.

The usual definition of institutional racism in the UK is that developed by the Macpherson inquiry into the Metropolitan Police following its failure to investigate the racially-motivated murder of a young black man from South London, Steven Lawrence, properly. That definition is:

> "The collective failure of an organisation to provide an appropriate and professional service to people because of their colour, culture, or ethnic origin. It can be seen or detected in processes, attitudes and behaviour which amount to discrimination through unwitting prejudice, ignorance, thoughtlessness and racist stereotyping which disadvantage minority ethnic people.[165]"

Obviously, to accuse an organisation of institutional racism is not the same as saying that the individuals who make up that organisation are racist: Macpherson makes that absolutely clear in the report (which amounts to a rebuttal of the argument, widely used in the police service before the Macpherson Report, that all one needs to do is to weed out "the bad apples" to deal with racism). The key point, emphasised by Macpherson, is that the victims of racism must be listened to and that their experience is a crucial factor in determining whether an organisation is

---

[164]   https://www.theguardian.com/society/2016/dec/12/antisemitism-definition-government-combat-hate-crime-jews-israel

[165]

https://assets.publishing.service.gov.uk/government/uploads/system/uploads/attachment_data/file/277111/4262.pdf operating in a racist way. The Macpherson principles have been universally accepted as an approach to defining and dealing with institutional racism.

It is difficult to see how the Labour Party would have treated any other ethnic minority in a similar way – whether it would have ignored the Macpherson principles and insisted on telling Jews what constitutes antisemitism, rather than listening to them; and to defy the Macpherson definition of institutional racism by continuing to assert that "there is no place for antisemites" within the Labour Party and relying on disciplinary processes to deal with Labour's equivalent of those "bad apples". In fact, it is notable that the Chakrabarti report[166], commissioned as an initial response to accusations of antisemitism within the Labour Party, focusses principally on disciplinary issues and does not mention the definition of antisemitism – IHRA or otherwise – at all; it is self-congratulatory about the Labour Party's record on minority rights in a way that often avoids discussing antisemitism as a separate phenomenon at all. Unsurprisingly, the report was criticised by Jewish groups inside and outside the Labour Party as a whitewash[167].

It is also notable that high-profile expulsions from the Labour Party of those accused of antisemitism – notably Tony Greenstein and Marc Wadsworth – have not been on the grounds of antisemitism *per se*, but for other unacceptable behaviours; and Ken Livingstone, whose comments on Hitler and Zionism were regarded by many as a test case for whether Labour was serious in dealing with antisemitism, resigned from the Party before any disciplinary proceedings were taken. There remain persistent allegations that senior Party figures – including members of Labour's National Executive Committee – have been complicit in supporting and providing assistance to those who have been accused of antisemitism[168].

---

[166]   https://labour.org.uk/wp-content/uploads/2017/10/Chakrabarti-Inquiry-Report-30June16.pdf

[167]   https://antisemitism.uk/the-chakrabarti-inquiry-is-a-vague-meaningless-whitewash-that-will-do-nothing-to-rid-labour-of-antisemitism/

[168]   https://www.huffingtonpost.co.uk/entry/christine-shawcroft-labour-anti-semitism-row-jeremy-corbyn_uk_5abe55e5e4b055e50acd2b12

To illustrate how the problem remains, in August 2018, a group of people within the Labour Party started an open letter to ask the NEC *not* to adopt all the examples of antisemitic behaviour in the IHRA definition[169]. It is worth deconstructing the arguments in that letter, because they are revealing about the politics of antisemitism in the Labour Party.

The letter claims that the adoption of the IHRA examples will lead to two problems. First, the adoption of the example involving a requirement that Israel should be held to a higher standard than any other democratic nation is wrong because, first, Israel is not a democratic nation in the accepted sense of the word and, secondly, because the adoption of that example could lead to the "outlawing" of the Boycott, Disinvestment and Sanctions (BDS) movement, which – the letter claims – is based on the methods of the anti-Apartheid movement. The letter argues that Israel is an apartheid state and should be treated as such. Second, the letter claims that example concerning denying the Jewish people the right to self-determination by, for example, claiming that the existence of the State of Israel is a racist endeavour could be used to close down legitimate public debate – going on to argue that the state of Israel was created through a process of ethnic cleansing; it suggests a moral equivalence between the Holocaust and the processes that led to the creation of Israel.

The latter point seems difficult to square with the Labour Party's official position of supporting a two-state solution to the Israel/Palestine issue, but, more importantly, seems to be calculated to allow the continuation of precisely the behaviour that has led to Labour's antisemitism crisis; its aim is not to improve the IHRA definition but to ensure that it does not prevent business as usual.

And ultimately this letter begs the same question as Holocaust denial. The point about Holocaust denial is that it is, at heart, a refusal to accept the existence of one of the most thoroughly-documented events in human history. There is no legitimate factual dispute over the Holocaust – the only reason anyone would want to deny it is ideological, to obscure the facts in the name of a post-factual ideology. And, similarly, why would people campaign to deny the adoption by Labour of the IHRA definition, which is widely-recognised throughout the world and which is advocated by the majority of Jewish groups? Again, the *only* answer is ideological. There is no evidence – none whatsoever – that, for example, the adoption of the

---

[169]   https://lettertolabournec.wordpress.com/2018/08/11/open-letter-to-the-national-executive-committee-of-the-labour-party/

IHRA definition by the Labour Government in Wales has closed down discussion of the Palestine issue in Wales; it's important to bear in mind that these are examples, provided as guidance and for information rather than as strict terms of regulation. The position in the open letter, couched in terms of freedom of expression, is hypothetical, unevidenced and purely unethical. It is not difficult to see why it could be easily construed as a device to ensure that antisemites can continue to undertake their activities without challenge on the grounds of racism. In their evocation of "free speech" the authors and signatories to that letter seem to me to be closer to the position of the alt-Right, seeking to justify hate-speech as a fundamental right, than I suspect they would ever care to admit.

And this attitude remains at the heart of Labour's antisemitism problem. At every stage the Party's leadership appears to have dug itself deeper into a hole of its own making; by refusing to adopt the full IHRA definition in the first place and choosing to lecture Jewish people on what constitutes antisemitism; by its continuing and increasingly tortuous special pleading and increasingly bizarre responses to, for example, the allegations that Jeremy Corbyn was involved in a wreath-laying ceremony for the people behind the massacre of Israeli athletes at the Munich Olympics in 1972[170]. One could be forgiven for thinking that we are a long way from the straight talking and honest politics promised when Corbyn became Labour leader, a little over three years beforehand.

The Labour Party leadership's reaction to these events looks, at first sight, like sheer incompetence; the incompetence of picking fights it can't win and becoming increasingly defensive when it is challenged. But the bigger problem is that these responses are not concerned with wider opinion but with squaring and internal debate. The Labour Party leadership cannot condemn antisemitism wholeheartedly, or adopt the IHRA in full, or conduct a civil dialogue with leaders of the Jewish community[171] – even though any one of those things would have helped it find a way through this crisis – because it is looking inward, at its own support base, and its own ideological tenets, rather than outwards to the people that it needs to convince to support it in order win an election and to form a Government.

And this brings us back to the example above of that mural in Tower Hamlets. Jeremy Corbyn appears not to have understood why it was antisemitic and grossly

170   https://www.theguardian.com/politics/2018/aug/13/jeremy-corbyn-not-involved-munich-olympics-massacre-wreath-laying

171   https://www.theguardian.com/politics/2018/apr/24/jewish-leaders-dismiss-corbyn-meeting-on-antisemitism-as-missed-opportunity

offensive; but the point is that the Labour Party, which has always placed political education at the heart of its methods and agenda, ought to know better. It claims to be an anti-racist party and in many respects has a powerful record of opposing racism; but it simply has not been willing, in recent years at least, to regard antisemitism as a fully-fledged form of racism. And in that sense it is institutionally antisemitic.

The problem, then, is at every level the Labour Party is unwilling to take Jewish opinion seriously; it simply does not appear to regard antisemitism as straightforward racism, placing it – whether intentionally or not – in a different category to other racisms. It is incapable of moving away from the antisemitic trope that criticising the Party for institutional antisemitism is some sort of plot, a conspiracy by people who want to undermine Corbyn's leadership and the prospects of a Corbyn-led Labour government.

So, what does the continuing saga of antisemitism within the Labour Party – still a long way from being resolved at the time of writing, tell us about the political method and practice of Corbyn's Labour Party?

It tells us that the Labour leadership cannot see beyond its bubble, and that it cannot reach out to and compromise with people outside that bubble. In other words, it represents a fundamental political failing. It talks about conducting politics for the many but remains in ideological hock to the few, people who – as I argued in Chapter [x] above, are more interested in the politics of position than achievement.

In conclusion, I do not wish to argue that Jeremy Corbyn is, necessarily, personally, an antisemite. I do believe that his behaviour has been naïve, ignorant and ill-informed, reflecting a refusal to open his mind and understand people outside the immediate political bubble in which he has spent his entire political career. In other words, I believe it epitomises what I regard as his personal political failings and I believe it raises serious questions about his judgement – and his fitness to hold the high office to which he aspires.

But I have no doubts whatsoever that Corbyn's Labour is institutionally antisemitic, and that that antisemitism is one of the defining features of what the Labour Party has become. It is not an unfortunate accident or the infiltration of an alien set of values into the tendency that has gained ideological control of Labour; it epitomises the values that underpin the values of the Leadership. It is absolutely implicit in their political method and will only be eradicated when the Party more widely chooses to reject that method.   I believe that it has failed to recognise or understand the feelings of Jewish people, to understand their concerns about the language and ideological positioning that is the norm within the Labour leadership. It has, to put it at is simplest, refused to show empathy.

CONCLUSION

The political scene in the Labour Party at the time of writing is fluid and, as I mentioned at the outset, many of the issues raised in this book are a very long way from being resolved. However, taking into account both the theoretical and practical issues described in this book, it is possible to form a clear picture of what Corbynism is.

First, it is a reaction to a particular set of circumstances in the Labour Party. As we saw in Chapters 2 and 3, it represents a response to a set of policy failures in the Labour Party, especially in opposition; and the circumstances of the election allowed Corbyn to portray himself as the authentic voice of Labour, rather than as a voice on its fringe. In many ways, his position on the political fringe was an advantage; it meant he was not associated with the Labour Party's failures, with the wider disillusionment with the political system, while allowing him to exploit the thirst for novelty and the unconventional that drives the torrent of material produced each day on social media. Although he was supported overwhelmingly by people who used the £3 supporter system to take part in the leadership election, he was the clear winner among long-term full members too. One reason for this was that, after a long period when Labour members felt they had had to hold themselves back emotionally and compromise on their basic political instincts, Corbyn was able to make a strong emotional connection with those instincts and – in the fact of a traumatic and comprehensive election defeat in 2015 – give people a sense of hope, that the dreams of a Labour landslide on an uncompromisingly radical could be achieved.

There appears to be universal agreement that the Labour Party has changed – and, on the basis of the arguments I set out in Chapter 2, it badly needed to change. But the Labour Party that has emerged after three years of Corbyn's leadership is a curious mix.

On the one hand, it has at its organizational heart a group of people drawn from the old ideological Left – especially the people who form the team immediately surrounding Corbyn - who seek to operate a fundamentally Leninist model of party organization. While it talks of being a "member-led" party, it favours a model in which there is a vanguard of committed supporters at the centre, directing the activities of the Party as a whole; and in which party democracy is used as a post-hoc rationalisation of the edicts of a central command. Many key staffers at the centre of Corbyn's project come directly from a mainstream Communist Party background, and continue to favour the tightly-controlled political structures that such a background entails. The tensions inherent in the conflict between member-led democracy and democratic centralism in fact are beginning to become clear, for example within Momentum over Brexit and between Momentum and the Labour Representation Committee over selection of slates for the NEC.

On the other hand, the wider surge in membership – which draws on the same demographic as before 2015 - is more a matter of entitled hobbyism than political engagement. This is reflected in the fact that Corbynism remains, at heart, a politics of individual position-taking, of virtue-signalling and a refusal to reach out beyond its own bubble; but also in the intense cult-like loyalty that is paid to Jeremy Corbyn as leader. At heart it is a politics of disengagement; and to that extent is completely consistent with the political initiative remaining in the hands of a tightly-kint and ideologically-committed central command.

That hobbyism is reflected in the fact that in many respects, Corbynism is not particularly radical; and that many of the key political positions of the Corbyn Labour, like rail privatization or the abolition of tuition fees, benefit the middle classes most. Aneurin Bevan wrote that the language of priorities is the religion of socialism; the iconic priorities of Corbynism make it clear where those priorities lie. The exception, as we have seen, is the idea of state ownership; but even here there is significant confusion over what ownership is *for* – there is no clear sense of objectives. And it is all of a piece with the politics of disengagement that there is no sense that changing ownership does not mean that difficult policy conflicts go away.

Most of all, Corbynism is firmly in the camp of post-truth politics. It rests at its heart on a relativist and, in the broadest sense, postmodern set of philosophical assumptions that rejects an empirical grounded truth-based politics in favour of a politics of competing narratives in an environment in which truth is a social or cultural construct, not a matter for empirically-grounded enquiry. It is a politics that is deeply reified. And as such, it is a long way from being a radical or liberating form of political discourse.

For all of these reasons, Corbynism is almost an apolitical phenomenon; it is as much about the emotional self-indulgence of Corbyn's supporters as any political commitment. There is a considerable amount of virtue-signalling and a need for a form of political expression for a generation – and for people in general – who feel that they have been left behind. But what it most certainly is not is about the rationale of generating real change from a rational political activity while building an evidence-based consensus.

The faithful know what they are against – it includes such reified terms as "austerity" and "neoliberalism" (although there seems to be little appetite to offer definitions of these slippery, and in the case of the latter, difficult and multifaceted things). But what are they for? It's actually quite difficult to know; there are policy pronouncements, there is talk of "defending the manifesto" (although such talk appears to ignore the fact that the 2017 election manifesto was – as we have seen - far from being a radical document).

But there isn't a narrative, a clear statement of values or a coherent programme for government; and the many rallies, the rousing choruses of "Oh Jeremy Corbyn", the parading of icons at Labour Conference, and vacuous slogans like "for the many" (a phrase that could have been adopted by any of the populist authoritarians of the modern world) are no substitute for these things. Where there are specific policy commitments – on renationalising the railways, on abolishing student fees, even on abolishing car park charges at hospitals – it's indicative, as we have seen, that these iconic policies are actually about redistributing, not to the poorest in society, but to the comfortable middle; far from being for the many, they're actually for the relatively privileged. Corbynism looks more like a matter of brand loyalty than a political movement.

And that disengagement seems to me to be central to the strategy of those closer to the centre of the Corbynist Labour Party, those who do have a clear ideological agenda – because their structural model of how the Party should function is essentially a Leninist one in which the role of the grass-roots member is not to drive political initiatives, but to provide endorsement and political cover for them. My own experience is that some of the most trenchant critics of the Corbynist model of party structure are ex-Militants, who saw this programme in action in the 1980s.

Nevertheless, it remains almost a truism that one cannot responsibly entrust power to a movement or tendency that, while desperate to obtain power, cannot frame a coherent narrative – beyond a handful of quite empty generalisations –

around what they would seek to do with it. And that is particularly pertinent when you have a political movement that appears incapable of thinking politically.

Perhaps the most important thing to understand about Corbynism is that it stands alongside Trump, Farage and Brexit as a symptom of post-truth politics. Its cultism, its institutional antisemitism, its obvious populism, its demonisation of liberalism and the politics of empirical rationalism, its claim to be "for the many" when it is proposes a political methodology that in truth empowers the few, and its embrace of personal demonisation as a political method – all of these place it alongside the most illiberal movements of our age. It is not a radical or empowering movement; its central ideology is precisely the opposite. Its privileging of position-taking and grandstanding over achievement marks it out as a tendency rooted in the neoliberal politics of personal satisfaction rather than the politics of personal endeavour; a politics of privilged individuals signalling their virtue in order to feel good about themselves, to comfort themselves with the illusion of being on the right side of history, rather than a politics of progress and achievement, based on a common grounded narrative that can appeal to – and for – the many.

And it is a powerful reminder that the real political divide today is not between left and right so much as between liberal, empirical, democratic politics and authoritarian populism; and that is a fault line that runs right through the middle of the British Labour Party. Labour was established as – and at its best has always been – a party of liberal and empirical social democracy; those who (rightly) laud the achievements of the post-war Attlee government should understand that it was, at its heart, always a government with social democracy at its core.

Speaking personally, it matters because, as a democratic socialist, I believe that the values of the Labour Party are more badly needed now than ever – an politics that brings engages empiricism and builds grounded narratives in pursuit of values of fairness and equality – and that challenges the reified ideological narratives around austerity. Corbynism represents a genuine expression of the need for change – but the fact remains that as a movement it is simply incapable – politically, intellectually, morally and even emotionally – of facing up to those challenge; because, as we have seen, it shares many of the same implicit assumptions about political activity as the ideological Right. What democratic socialists need to do now is to build a grounded narrative, a social democratic narrative based in reason, experience and argument, as to how we can construct a different society. And to do that you need to reach out and engage; but, as I have emphasised in this book, Corbynism is at heart a philosophy of disengagement, wrapped in its own ideological world of dogma facilitated through privileged hobbyism

Again speaking personally I suppose the fact that angers me most about the Corbynist movement is its sheer political frivolity. I live in the Western suburbs of Cardiff – a resonably affluent enclave within half-an-hour's drive of what are officially recognised by the EU as some of the poorest communities in Europe, and less than a mile from Ely, where riots erupted in 1991 – over bread[172]. Places in which one in four young adults are unemployed – and from which those young people fortunate enough to get a university education almost always leave and almost never return. Places where a third of children live in poverty, inherently disadvantaged before they even start out in life; places that voted to leave the EU but where the funding for preventative child safeguarding is largely comes from EU match funding. Places that voted for Brexit because the Remain campaign lacked the imagination in 2016 to realise that asking people in the poorest communities effectively to vote for the status quo was doomed to failure in places that had never recovered from the economic catastrophes visited on them by Margaret Thatcher in the 1980s.

And yet, at my own Constituency Labour Party meeting, I heard, shortly after the EU referendum, a prominent Corbynist supporter claiming that the cause of that leave vote was that people from "the valleys[173]" were "uneducated and bigoted" (to the fury of my Rhondda-born, Oxford University-educated partner, with two postgraduate degrees to her name). When challenged, the Constituency officers made half-hearted noises about how the comment wasn't to be taken seriously, before locking themselves down in denial.

As far as "the valleys" are concerned, our Corbynist speaker might have reflected that Keir Hardie was elected as the first ever Labour MP just a few miles north of here, in the Merthyr Tydfil and Aberdare constituency, in 1900, by the forebears of those bigoted and uneducated voters of 2016.

But this cannot be dismissed as the view of one rather ill-informed individual. On the contrary, it is a comment that is all of a piece with the arrogance and frivolity of the Corbyn supporters in Wales. First, it is simplistic: it demonstrates an inability to engage with the detail of politics, and to understand that people's motivations are

---

[172] https://www.bbc.co.uk/news/uk-wales-south-east-wales-37183995

[173] One of the first things you learn, when you move to South Wales, is that it's regarded as patronising to talk about "the valleys". People come from the Rhondda Valley, the Cynon Valley and so on, but never "the valleys".

complex and often difficult to unravel; it is sadly typical of the London politician's easy and often profoundly prejudiced failure to engage with Wales and its politics.

Moreover: here, in one of the poorest parts of Europe, the main concerns of the Corbyn-supporting left have, as I mentioned earlier, not been inequality, the thousands of the most vulnerable people in Wales forced into destitution through the introduction of Universal Credit, or the catastrophic effect that Brexit – of any flavour – will have on jobs and living standards in Wales; it has been the esoteric question of how to elect the leader of Welsh Labour, even before Carwyn Jones announced his intention to stand down at the end of 2018. It is the internal structures of Labour in Wales, and the need to capture them for Corbyn, that really motivates and excites Corbyn's Welsh cohorts. One may well conclude that this matters (although it appears wholly to undermine the "clear red water" strategy of former First Minister Rhodri Morgan, who sought to place distance between Labour in Wales and Westminster, this avoiding the accusations of being a Westminster branch office that caused such enormous damage to Labour in Scotland), but I suspect that those at the sharp end of austerity might conclude that there are other, more important things for a political party that claims to act "for the many" to campaign about. Operating in its small isolation chamber, it cannot understand that questions of Labour internal politics are of little or no interest to those who who rely on food banks to feed their children; it is the politics of privilege, pure and simple. The Corbynist faction that dominates my local Labour Party would have been all too familiar to the Orwell of *The Road to Wigan Pier*.

And in Wales we have the opportunity to make the comparison; because the Corbynist Left stands in contrast to a Government that, in the face of austerity from Westminster, has sought to protect services for the most vulnerable and to bring jobs and prosperity to Wales. Labour in England recently announced its intention to bring back Education Maintenance Allowance, to help those from lower-income backgrounds, to stay in education[174]; Labour in Wales kept it when it was abolished in England. At a time when Sure Start provision has been savagely cut in England, Carwyn Jones has placed childcare and early years at the heart of his political agenda. And Carwyn Jones, has led Welsh Labour to two national election victories, in 2011 and 2016 – and in that second election campaign could honestly claim that every single commitment of his 2011 manifesto had been implemented. Ultimately, we are back with the distinction we discussed in Chapter 4; that the politics of Corbynism is politics of positioning, not the practical politics of achievement and delivery. Which is more likely to deliver for the most vulnerable in our society?

---

[174] https://www.tes.com/news/labour-calls-government-bring-back-ema

In 1931, the great Socialist thinker and historian R H Tawney wrote a pamphlet entitled "The Choices before the Labour Party", an excoriating attack on Ramsay MacDonald's new national government. He called for a Labour Party that was strong in its values and remained an effective voice for the people it represented. "To kick over an idol", he wrote, "you must first get up off your knees". As we face the inadequacies of Corbynism as a political project, it is surely time for all of us who call ourselves democratic socialists to follow Tawney's lead.

SELECT BIBLIOGRAPHY

Adonis, Andrew *Five Days in May: The Coalition and beyond* (2013) London: Biteback Press

Anderson, Perry *The Origins of Postmodernity* (1998) London; Verso

Arendt, Hannah, *The Origins of Totalitarianism* (1951) London: Penguin

Bevan, Aneurin *In Place of Fear* (1961 edn) London: MacGibbon and Kee

Brown, Gordon *My Life, Our Times* (2017) London: The Bodley Head

Butler, Christopher *Postmodernism: A Very Short Introduction* (2002) Oxford: Oxford University Press

Chomsky, Noam and Herman, Edward S *Manufacturing Consent: The Political Economy of the Mass Media* (2010) Vintage digital

Crick, Bernard *In Defence of Politics* (5th edn) (2013) London: Bloomsbury

Crick, Michael *Militant* (1984, rev 2016) London: Biteback

Dillow, Chris *The End of Politics – New Labour and the folly of managerialism* (2007) Petersfield: Harriman House

Eagleton, Terry *After Theory* (2004) London: Penguin

Eagleton, Terry *Marx* (1997) London: Phoenix

Eribon, Didier *Michel Foucault* (1992) London: Faber

Harvey, David *A Brief History of Neoliberalism* (2007) Oxford: Oxford University Press

Havel, Vaclav *Living in Truth* (1989) London: Faber

Hirsch, David *Contemporary Left Antisemitism* (2017) London: Routledge

Lenin, V I *Left Wing Communism – an infantile disorder?* (1920)
https://www.marxists.org/archive/lenin/works/1920/lwc/

Lenin V I *What is to be done?* (1902)
https://www.marxists.org/archive/lenin/works/1901/witbd/

Magee, Bryan *Popper* (1982) London: Fontana Modern Masters

Marx, Karl abridged and edited McLellan, David *Capital* (1995) Oxford: Oxford University Press

Mason, Paul *Postcapitalism* (2015) London: Allen Lane

McLellan, David *Marx* (2nd ed) (1975) London: Fontana

McLellan, David *Karl Marx: A Biography* (1995) London: Macmillan

Miliband, Ralph *Parliamentary Socialism* (2009 – 2nd revised edition) London: The Merlin Press

Orwell, George *The Road to Wigan Pier*

Popper, Karl *The Open Society and its Enemies* (2 vols, 1944) London: Routledge

Prince, Rosa Comrade Corbyn

Seymour, Richard *Corbyn: The strange rebirth of radical politics* (2nd Ed) (2017) London: Verso

Singer, Peter *Hegel* (1983) Oxford: Oxford University Press

Tawney, R H: *The Choices before the Labour Party* (1931) in *The Attack and Other Papers* (1983) London: Spokesman